C-631   CAREER EXAMINATION SERIES

This is your
PASSBOOK for...

Public Health Nurse

Test Preparation Study Guide
Questions & Answers

COPYRIGHT NOTICE

This book is SOLELY intended for, is sold ONLY to, and its use is RESTRICTED to individual, bona fide applicants or candidates who qualify by virtue of having seriously filed applications for appropriate license, certificate, professional and/or promotional advancement, higher school matriculation, scholarship, or other legitimate requirements of education and/or governmental authorities.

This book is NOT intended for use, class instruction, tutoring, training, duplication, copying, reprinting, excerption, or adaptation, etc., by:

1) Other publishers
2) Proprietors and/or Instructors of "Coaching" and/or Preparatory Courses
3) Personnel and/or Training Divisions of commercial, industrial, and governmental organizations
4) Schools, colleges, or universities and/or their departments and staffs, including teachers and other personnel
5) Testing Agencies or Bureaus
6) Study groups which seek by the purchase of a single volume to copy and/or duplicate and/or adapt this material for use by the group as a whole without having purchased individual volumes for each of the members of the group
7) Et al.

Such persons would be in violation of appropriate Federal and State statutes.

PROVISION OF LICENSING AGREEMENTS – Recognized educational, commercial, industrial, and governmental institutions and organizations, and others legitimately engaged in educational pursuits, including training, testing, and measurement activities, may address request for a licensing agreement to the copyright owners, who will determine whether, and under what conditions, including fees and charges, the materials in this book may be used them. In other words, a licensing facility exists for the legitimate use of the material in this book on other than an individual basis. However, it is asseverated and affirmed here that the material in this book CANNOT be used without the receipt of the express permission of such a licensing agreement from the Publishers. Inquiries re licensing should be addressed to the company, attention rights and permissions department.

All rights reserved, including the right of reproduction in whole or in part, in any form or by any means, electronic or mechanical, including photocopying, recording, or by any information storage and retrieval system, without permission in writing from the Publisher.

Copyright © 2024 by
National Learning Corporation

212 Michael Drive, Syosset, NY 11791
(516) 921-8888 • www.passbooks.com
E-mail: info@passbooks.com

PUBLISHED IN THE UNITED STATES OF AMERICA

PASSBOOK® SERIES

THE *PASSBOOK® SERIES* has been created to prepare applicants and candidates for the ultimate academic battlefield – the examination room.

At some time in our lives, each and every one of us may be required to take an examination – for validation, matriculation, admission, qualification, registration, certification, or licensure.

Based on the assumption that every applicant or candidate has met the basic formal educational standards, has taken the required number of courses, and read the necessary texts, the *PASSBOOK® SERIES* furnishes the one special preparation which may assure passing with confidence, instead of failing with insecurity. Examination questions – together with answers – are furnished as the basic vehicle for study so that the mysteries of the examination and its compounding difficulties may be eliminated or diminished by a sure method.

This book is meant to help you pass your examination provided that you qualify and are serious in your objective.

The entire field is reviewed through the huge store of content information which is succinctly presented through a provocative and challenging approach – the question-and-answer method.

A climate of success is established by furnishing the correct answers at the end of each test.

You soon learn to recognize types of questions, forms of questions, and patterns of questioning. You may even begin to anticipate expected outcomes.

You perceive that many questions are repeated or adapted so that you can gain acute insights, which may enable you to score many sure points.

You learn how to confront new questions, or types of questions, and to attack them confidently and work out the correct answers.

You note objectives and emphases, and recognize pitfalls and dangers, so that you may make positive educational adjustments.

Moreover, you are kept fully informed in relation to new concepts, methods, practices, and directions in the field.

You discover that you are actually taking the examination all the time: you are preparing for the examination by "taking" an examination, not by reading extraneous and/or supererogatory textbooks.

In short, this PASSBOOK®, used directedly, should be an important factor in helping you to pass your test.

PUBLIC HEALTH NURSE

DUTIES AND RESPONSIBILITIES:
Under supervision, performs public health nursing functions in a generalized public health nursing program which includes clinics, schools, and home nursing.

WHAT THE JOB IS LIKE:
The work involves responsibility for the performance of public health nursing activities with individuals, families, clinics and classes in accordance with the planned program of the agency. This is a specialized area of professional nursing practiced within the outlines of organized community health. The Public Health Nurse has the responsibility for assessing the health care needs of patients and families, providing professional nursing care where necessary and teaching families health principles for prevention of disease and maintenance of health. Work is performed under the supervision of a Supervising Public Health Nurse. Incumbents do related work as required.

EXAMPLES OF TYPICAL TASKS
Administers routine screening tests; interprets, evaluates, and reports the results; counsels patients or family on results of diagnostic tests, treatment procedures, and medication prescribed; administers oral and topical medications, therapeutic injections and immunization, being alert and watchful for adverse side effects or reactions; maintains medical charts and records on patients; teaches patients and family about nutrition, hygiene, prevention, rehabilitation, and community resources available; maintains community resource file, makes referrals to other agencies, acts as patient advocate and follows up; controls, keeps an inventory, and orders supplies; insures proper labeling, security, and storage of medications and specimens; supervises and/or coordinates delivery of services with other health-care personnel; assigns work, supervises activities, and evaluates performance of subordinates; sets up, coordinates, and implements delivery of required health-care practices in the public and parochial school systems; answers requests for interpretation, and explanation on department of health policies and regulations, and general information on public health matters; makes home visits to follow up on patients, school students, and their families; gathers information on sudden infant deaths (SIDS), window-fall accidents, lead poisoning and unregistered home births; observes and reports environmental and/or sociological health hazards; and writes narrative reports on activities.

SUBJECT OF EXAMINATION
The test will be of the multiple-choice type and will contain questions relating to the duties above, and medical and nursing knowledge necessary to the position.

HOW TO TAKE A TEST

I. YOU MUST PASS AN EXAMINATION

A. WHAT EVERY CANDIDATE SHOULD KNOW

Examination applicants often ask us for help in preparing for the written test. What can I study in advance? What kinds of questions will be asked? How will the test be given? How will the papers be graded?

As an applicant for a civil service examination, you may be wondering about some of these things. Our purpose here is to suggest effective methods of advance study and to describe civil service examinations.

Your chances for success on this examination can be increased if you know how to prepare. Those "pre-examination jitters" can be reduced if you know what to expect. You can even experience an adventure in good citizenship if you know why civil service exams are given.

B. WHY ARE CIVIL SERVICE EXAMINATIONS GIVEN?

Civil service examinations are important to you in two ways. As a citizen, you want public jobs filled by employees who know how to do their work. As a job seeker, you want a fair chance to compete for that job on an equal footing with other candidates. The best-known means of accomplishing this two-fold goal is the competitive examination.

Exams are widely publicized throughout the nation. They may be administered for jobs in federal, state, city, municipal, town or village governments or agencies.

Any citizen may apply, with some limitations, such as the age or residence of applicants. Your experience and education may be reviewed to see whether you meet the requirements for the particular examination. When these requirements exist, they are reasonable and applied consistently to all applicants. Thus, a competitive examination may cause you some uneasiness now, but it is your privilege and safeguard.

C. HOW ARE CIVIL SERVICE EXAMS DEVELOPED?

Examinations are carefully written by trained technicians who are specialists in the field known as "psychological measurement," in consultation with recognized authorities in the field of work that the test will cover. These experts recommend the subject matter areas or skills to be tested; only those knowledges or skills important to your success on the job are included. The most reliable books and source materials available are used as references. Together, the experts and technicians judge the difficulty level of the questions.

Test technicians know how to phrase questions so that the problem is clearly stated. Their ethics do not permit "trick" or "catch" questions. Questions may have been tried out on sample groups, or subjected to statistical analysis, to determine their usefulness.

Written tests are often used in combination with performance tests, ratings of training and experience, and oral interviews. All of these measures combine to form the best-known means of finding the right person for the right job.

II. HOW TO PASS THE WRITTEN TEST

A. NATURE OF THE EXAMINATION

To prepare intelligently for civil service examinations, you should know how they differ from school examinations you have taken. In school you were assigned certain definite pages to read or subjects to cover. The examination questions were quite detailed and usually emphasized memory. Civil service exams, on the other hand, try to discover your present ability to perform the duties of a position, plus your potentiality to learn these duties. In other words, a civil service exam attempts to predict how successful you will be. Questions cover such a broad area that they cannot be as minute and detailed as school exam questions.

In the public service similar kinds of work, or positions, are grouped together in one "class." This process is known as *position-classification*. All the positions in a class are paid according to the salary range for that class. One class title covers all of these positions, and they are all tested by the same examination.

B. FOUR BASIC STEPS

1) Study the announcement

How, then, can you know what subjects to study? Our best answer is: "Learn as much as possible about the class of positions for which you've applied." The exam will test the knowledge, skills and abilities needed to do the work.

Your most valuable source of information about the position you want is the official exam announcement. This announcement lists the training and experience qualifications. Check these standards and apply only if you come reasonably close to meeting them.

The brief description of the position in the examination announcement offers some clues to the subjects which will be tested. Think about the job itself. Review the duties in your mind. Can you perform them, or are there some in which you are rusty? Fill in the blank spots in your preparation.

Many jurisdictions preview the written test in the exam announcement by including a section called "Knowledge and Abilities Required," "Scope of the Examination," or some similar heading. Here you will find out specifically what fields will be tested.

2) Review your own background

Once you learn in general what the position is all about, and what you need to know to do the work, ask yourself which subjects you already know fairly well and which need improvement. You may wonder whether to concentrate on improving your strong areas or on building some background in your fields of weakness. When the announcement has specified "some knowledge" or "considerable knowledge," or has used adjectives like "beginning principles of..." or "advanced ... methods," you can get a clue as to the number and difficulty of questions to be asked in any given field. More questions, and hence broader coverage, would be included for those subjects which are more important in the work. Now weigh your strengths and weaknesses against the job requirements and prepare accordingly.

3) Determine the level of the position

Another way to tell how intensively you should prepare is to understand the level of the job for which you are applying. Is it the entering level? In other words, is this the position in which beginners in a field of work are hired? Or is it an intermediate or advanced level? Sometimes this is indicated by such words as "Junior" or "Senior" in the class title. Other jurisdictions use Roman numerals to designate the level – Clerk I, Clerk II, for example. The word "Supervisor" sometimes appears in the title. If the level is not indicated by the title, check the description of duties. Will you be working under very close supervision, or will you have responsibility for independent decisions in this work?

4) Choose appropriate study materials

Now that you know the subjects to be examined and the relative amount of each subject to be covered, you can choose suitable study materials. For beginning level jobs, or even advanced ones, if you have a pronounced weakness in some aspect of your training, read a modern, standard textbook in that field. Be sure it is up to date and has general coverage. Such books are normally available at your library, and the librarian will be glad to help you locate one. For entry-level positions, questions of appropriate difficulty are chosen — neither highly advanced questions, nor those too simple. Such questions require careful thought but not advanced training.

If the position for which you are applying is technical or advanced, you will read more advanced, specialized material. If you are already familiar with the basic principles of your field, elementary textbooks would waste your time. Concentrate on advanced textbooks and technical periodicals. Think through the concepts and review difficult problems in your field.

These are all general sources. You can get more ideas on your own initiative, following these leads. For example, training manuals and publications of the government agency which employs workers in your field can be useful, particularly for technical and professional positions. A letter or visit to the government department involved may result in more specific study suggestions, and certainly will provide you with a more definite idea of the exact nature of the position you are seeking.

III. KINDS OF TESTS

Tests are used for purposes other than measuring knowledge and ability to perform specified duties. For some positions, it is equally important to test ability to make adjustments to new situations or to profit from training. In others, basic mental abilities not dependent on information are essential. Questions which test these things may not appear as pertinent to the duties of the position as those which test for knowledge and information. Yet they are often highly important parts of a fair examination. For very general questions, it is almost impossible to help you direct your study efforts. What we can do is to point out some of the more common of these general abilities needed in public service positions and describe some typical questions.

1) General information

Broad, general information has been found useful for predicting job success in some kinds of work. This is tested in a variety of ways, from vocabulary lists to questions about current events. Basic background in some field of work, such as sociology or economics, may be sampled in a group of questions. Often these are principles which have become familiar to most persons through exposure rather than through formal training. It is difficult to advise you how to study for these questions; being alert to the world around you is our best suggestion.

2) Verbal ability

An example of an ability needed in many positions is verbal or language ability. Verbal ability is, in brief, the ability to use and understand words. Vocabulary and grammar tests are typical measures of this ability. Reading comprehension or paragraph interpretation questions are common in many kinds of civil service tests. You are given a paragraph of written material and asked to find its central meaning.

3) Numerical ability

Number skills can be tested by the familiar arithmetic problem, by checking paired lists of numbers to see which are alike and which are different, or by interpreting charts and graphs. In the latter test, a graph may be printed in the test booklet which you are asked to use as the basis for answering questions.

4) Observation

A popular test for law-enforcement positions is the observation test. A picture is shown to you for several minutes, then taken away. Questions about the picture test your ability to observe both details and larger elements.

5) Following directions

In many positions in the public service, the employee must be able to carry out written instructions dependably and accurately. You may be given a chart with several columns, each column listing a variety of information. The questions require you to carry out directions involving the information given in the chart.

6) Skills and aptitudes

Performance tests effectively measure some manual skills and aptitudes. When the skill is one in which you are trained, such as typing or shorthand, you can practice. These tests are often very much like those given in business school or high school courses. For many of the other skills and aptitudes, however, no short-time preparation can be made. Skills and abilities natural to you or that you have developed throughout your lifetime are being tested.

Many of the general questions just described provide all the data needed to answer the questions and ask you to use your reasoning ability to find the answers. Your best preparation for these tests, as well as for tests of facts and ideas, is to be at your physical and mental best. You, no doubt, have your own methods of getting into an exam-taking mood and keeping "in shape." The next section lists some ideas on this subject.

IV. KINDS OF QUESTIONS

Only rarely is the "essay" question, which you answer in narrative form, used in civil service tests. Civil service tests are usually of the short-answer type. Full instructions for answering these questions will be given to you at the examination. But in case this is your first experience with short-answer questions and separate answer sheets, here is what you need to know:

1) Multiple-choice Questions

Most popular of the short-answer questions is the "multiple choice" or "best answer" question. It can be used, for example, to test for factual knowledge, ability to solve problems or judgment in meeting situations found at work.

A multiple-choice question is normally one of three types—

- It can begin with an incomplete statement followed by several possible endings. You are to find the one ending which *best* completes the statement, although some of the others may not be entirely wrong.
- It can also be a complete statement in the form of a question which is answered by choosing one of the statements listed.

- It can be in the form of a problem – again you select the best answer.

Here is an example of a multiple-choice question with a discussion which should give you some clues as to the method for choosing the right answer:

When an employee has a complaint about his assignment, the action which will *best* help him overcome his difficulty is to
   A. discuss his difficulty with his coworkers
   B. take the problem to the head of the organization
   C. take the problem to the person who gave him the assignment
   D. say nothing to anyone about his complaint

In answering this question, you should study each of the choices to find which is best. Consider choice "A" – Certainly an employee may discuss his complaint with fellow employees, but no change or improvement can result, and the complaint remains unresolved. Choice "B" is a poor choice since the head of the organization probably does not know what assignment you have been given, and taking your problem to him is known as "going over the head" of the supervisor. The supervisor, or person who made the assignment, is the person who can clarify it or correct any injustice. Choice "C" is, therefore, correct. To say nothing, as in choice "D," is unwise. Supervisors have and interest in knowing the problems employees are facing, and the employee is seeking a solution to his problem.

2) True/False Questions

The "true/false" or "right/wrong" form of question is sometimes used. Here a complete statement is given. Your job is to decide whether the statement is right or wrong.

SAMPLE: A roaming cell-phone call to a nearby city costs less than a non-roaming call to a distant city.

This statement is wrong, or false, since roaming calls are more expensive.

This is not a complete list of all possible question forms, although most of the others are variations of these common types. You will always get complete directions for answering questions. Be sure you understand *how* to mark your answers – ask questions until you do.

V. RECORDING YOUR ANSWERS

Computer terminals are used more and more today for many different kinds of exams.
For an examination with very few applicants, you may be told to record your answers in the test booklet itself. Separate answer sheets are much more common. If this separate answer sheet is to be scored by machine – and this is often the case – it is highly important that you mark your answers correctly in order to get credit.

An electronic scoring machine is often used in civil service offices because of the speed with which papers can be scored. Machine-scored answer sheets must be marked with a pencil, which will be given to you. This pencil has a high graphite content which responds to the electronic scoring machine. As a matter of fact, stray dots may register as answers, so do not let your pencil rest on the answer sheet while you are pondering the correct answer. Also, if your pencil lead breaks or is otherwise defective, ask for another.

Since the answer sheet will be dropped in a slot in the scoring machine, be careful not to bend the corners or get the paper crumpled.

The answer sheet normally has five vertical columns of numbers, with 30 numbers to a column. These numbers correspond to the question numbers in your test booklet. After each number, going across the page are four or five pairs of dotted lines. These short dotted lines have small letters or numbers above them. The first two pairs may also have a "T" or "F" above the letters. This indicates that the first two pairs only are to be used if the questions are of the true-false type. If the questions are multiple choice, disregard the "T" and "F" and pay attention only to the small letters or numbers.

Answer your questions in the manner of the sample that follows:

32. The largest city in the United States is
    A. Washington, D.C.
    B. New York City
    C. Chicago
    D. Detroit
    E. San Francisco

1) Choose the answer you think is best. (New York City is the largest, so "B" is correct.)
2) Find the row of dotted lines numbered the same as the question you are answering. (Find row number 32)
3) Find the pair of dotted lines corresponding to the answer. (Find the pair of lines under the mark "B.")
4) Make a solid black mark between the dotted lines.

VI. BEFORE THE TEST

Common sense will help you find procedures to follow to get ready for an examination. Too many of us, however, overlook these sensible measures. Indeed, nervousness and fatigue have been found to be the most serious reasons why applicants fail to do their best on civil service tests. Here is a list of reminders:

- Begin your preparation early – Don't wait until the last minute to go scurrying around for books and materials or to find out what the position is all about.
- Prepare continuously – An hour a night for a week is better than an all-night cram session. This has been definitely established. What is more, a night a week for a month will return better dividends than crowding your study into a shorter period of time.
- Locate the place of the exam – You have been sent a notice telling you when and where to report for the examination. If the location is in a different town or otherwise unfamiliar to you, it would be well to inquire the best route and learn something about the building.
- Relax the night before the test – Allow your mind to rest. Do not study at all that night. Plan some mild recreation or diversion; then go to bed early and get a good night's sleep.
- Get up early enough to make a leisurely trip to the place for the test – This way unforeseen events, traffic snarls, unfamiliar buildings, etc. will not upset you.
- Dress comfortably – A written test is not a fashion show. You will be known by number and not by name, so wear something comfortable.

- Leave excess paraphernalia at home – Shopping bags and odd bundles will get in your way. You need bring only the items mentioned in the official notice you received; usually everything you need is provided. Do not bring reference books to the exam. They will only confuse those last minutes and be taken away from you when in the test room.
- Arrive somewhat ahead of time – If because of transportation schedules you must get there very early, bring a newspaper or magazine to take your mind off yourself while waiting.
- Locate the examination room – When you have found the proper room, you will be directed to the seat or part of the room where you will sit. Sometimes you are given a sheet of instructions to read while you are waiting. Do not fill out any forms until you are told to do so; just read them and be prepared.
- Relax and prepare to listen to the instructions
- If you have any physical problem that may keep you from doing your best, be sure to tell the test administrator. If you are sick or in poor health, you really cannot do your best on the exam. You can come back and take the test some other time.

VII. AT THE TEST

The day of the test is here and you have the test booklet in your hand. The temptation to get going is very strong. Caution! There is more to success than knowing the right answers. You must know how to identify your papers and understand variations in the type of short-answer question used in this particular examination. Follow these suggestions for maximum results from your efforts:

1) Cooperate with the monitor

The test administrator has a duty to create a situation in which you can be as much at ease as possible. He will give instructions, tell you when to begin, check to see that you are marking your answer sheet correctly, and so on. He is not there to guard you, although he will see that your competitors do not take unfair advantage. He wants to help you do your best.

2) Listen to all instructions

Don't jump the gun! Wait until you understand all directions. In most civil service tests you get more time than you need to answer the questions. So don't be in a hurry. Read each word of instructions until you clearly understand the meaning. Study the examples, listen to all announcements and follow directions. Ask questions if you do not understand what to do.

3) Identify your papers

Civil service exams are usually identified by number only. You will be assigned a number; you must not put your name on your test papers. Be sure to copy your number correctly. Since more than one exam may be given, copy your exact examination title.

4) Plan your time

Unless you are told that a test is a "speed" or "rate of work" test, speed itself is usually not important. Time enough to answer all the questions will be provided, but this does not mean that you have all day. An overall time limit has been set. Divide the total time (in minutes) by the number of questions to determine the approximate time you have for each question.

5) Do not linger over difficult questions

If you come across a difficult question, mark it with a paper clip (useful to have along) and come back to it when you have been through the booklet. One caution if you do this – be sure to skip a number on your answer sheet as well. Check often to be sure that you have not lost your place and that you are marking in the row numbered the same as the question you are answering.

6) Read the questions

Be sure you know what the question asks! Many capable people are unsuccessful because they failed to *read* the questions correctly.

7) Answer all questions

Unless you have been instructed that a penalty will be deducted for incorrect answers, it is better to guess than to omit a question.

8) Speed tests

It is often better NOT to guess on speed tests. It has been found that on timed tests people are tempted to spend the last few seconds before time is called in marking answers at random – without even reading them – in the hope of picking up a few extra points. To discourage this practice, the instructions may warn you that your score will be "corrected" for guessing. That is, a penalty will be applied. The incorrect answers will be deducted from the correct ones, or some other penalty formula will be used.

9) Review your answers

If you finish before time is called, go back to the questions you guessed or omitted to give them further thought. Review other answers if you have time.

10) Return your test materials

If you are ready to leave before others have finished or time is called, take ALL your materials to the monitor and leave quietly. Never take any test material with you. The monitor can discover whose papers are not complete, and taking a test booklet may be grounds for disqualification.

VIII. EXAMINATION TECHNIQUES

1) Read the general instructions carefully. These are usually printed on the first page of the exam booklet. As a rule, these instructions refer to the timing of the examination; the fact that you should not start work until the signal and must stop work at a signal, etc. If there are any *special* instructions, such as a choice of questions to be answered, make sure that you note this instruction carefully.

2) When you are ready to start work on the examination, that is as soon as the signal has been given, read the instructions to each question booklet, underline any key words or phrases, such as *least, best, outline, describe* and the like. In this way you will tend to answer as requested rather than discover on reviewing your paper that you *listed without describing*, that you selected the *worst* choice rather than the *best* choice, etc.

3) If the examination is of the objective or multiple-choice type – that is, each question will also give a series of possible answers: A, B, C or D, and you are called upon to select the best answer and write the letter next to that answer on your answer paper – it is advisable to start answering each question in turn. There may be anywhere from 50 to 100 such questions in the three or four hours allotted and you can see how much time would be taken if you read through all the questions before beginning to answer any. Furthermore, if you come across a question or group of questions which you know would be difficult to answer, it would undoubtedly affect your handling of all the other questions.

4) If the examination is of the essay type and contains but a few questions, it is a moot point as to whether you should read all the questions before starting to answer any one. Of course, if you are given a choice – say five out of seven and the like – then it is essential to read all the questions so you can eliminate the two that are most difficult. If, however, you are asked to answer all the questions, there may be danger in trying to answer the easiest one first because you may find that you will spend too much time on it. The best technique is to answer the first question, then proceed to the second, etc.

5) Time your answers. Before the exam begins, write down the time it started, then add the time allowed for the examination and write down the time it must be completed, then divide the time available somewhat as follows:
    - If 3-1/2 hours are allowed, that would be 210 minutes. If you have 80 objective-type questions, that would be an average of 2-1/2 minutes per question. Allow yourself no more than 2 minutes per question, or a total of 160 minutes, which will permit about 50 minutes to review.
    - If for the time allotment of 210 minutes there are 7 essay questions to answer, that would average about 30 minutes a question. Give yourself only 25 minutes per question so that you have about 35 minutes to review.

6) The most important instruction is to *read each question* and make sure you know what is wanted. The second most important instruction is to *time yourself properly* so that you answer every question. The third most important instruction is to *answer every question*. Guess if you have to but include something for each question. Remember that you will receive no credit for a blank and will probably receive some credit if you write something in answer to an essay question. If you guess a letter – say "B" for a multiple-choice question – you may have guessed right. If you leave a blank as an answer to a multiple-choice question, the examiners may respect your feelings but it will not add a point to your score. Some exams may penalize you for wrong answers, so in such cases *only*, you may not want to guess unless you have some basis for your answer.

7) Suggestions
    a. Objective-type questions
        1. Examine the question booklet for proper sequence of pages and questions
        2. Read all instructions carefully
        3. Skip any question which seems too difficult; return to it after all other questions have been answered
        4. Apportion your time properly; do not spend too much time on any single question or group of questions

5. Note and underline key words – *all, most, fewest, least, best, worst, same, opposite,* etc.
6. Pay particular attention to negatives
7. Note unusual option, e.g., unduly long, short, complex, different or similar in content to the body of the question
8. Observe the use of "hedging" words – *probably, may, most likely,* etc.
9. Make sure that your answer is put next to the same number as the question
10. Do not second-guess unless you have good reason to believe the second answer is definitely more correct
11. Cross out original answer if you decide another answer is more accurate; do not erase until you are ready to hand your paper in
12. Answer all questions; guess unless instructed otherwise
13. Leave time for review

b. Essay questions
1. Read each question carefully
2. Determine exactly what is wanted. Underline key words or phrases.
3. Decide on outline or paragraph answer
4. Include many different points and elements unless asked to develop any one or two points or elements
5. Show impartiality by giving pros and cons unless directed to select one side only
6. Make and write down any assumptions you find necessary to answer the questions
7. Watch your English, grammar, punctuation and choice of words
8. Time your answers; don't crowd material

8) Answering the essay question

Most essay questions can be answered by framing the specific response around several key words or ideas. Here are a few such key words or ideas:

M's: manpower, materials, methods, money, management
P's: purpose, program, policy, plan, procedure, practice, problems, pitfalls, personnel, public relations

  a. Six basic steps in handling problems:
    1. Preliminary plan and background development
    2. Collect information, data and facts
    3. Analyze and interpret information, data and facts
    4. Analyze and develop solutions as well as make recommendations
    5. Prepare report and sell recommendations
    6. Install recommendations and follow up effectiveness

  b. Pitfalls to avoid
    1. *Taking things for granted* – A statement of the situation does not necessarily imply that each of the elements is necessarily true; for example, a complaint may be invalid and biased so that all that can be taken for granted is that a complaint has been registered

2. *Considering only one side of a situation* – Wherever possible, indicate several alternatives and then point out the reasons you selected the best one
3. *Failing to indicate follow up* – Whenever your answer indicates action on your part, make certain that you will take proper follow-up action to see how successful your recommendations, procedures or actions turn out to be
4. *Taking too long in answering any single question* – Remember to time your answers properly

IX. AFTER THE TEST

Scoring procedures differ in detail among civil service jurisdictions although the general principles are the same. Whether the papers are hand-scored or graded by machine we have described, they are nearly always graded by number. That is, the person who marks the paper knows only the number – never the name – of the applicant. Not until all the papers have been graded will they be matched with names. If other tests, such as training and experience or oral interview ratings have been given, scores will be combined. Different parts of the examination usually have different weights. For example, the written test might count 60 percent of the final grade, and a rating of training and experience 40 percent. In many jurisdictions, veterans will have a certain number of points added to their grades.

After the final grade has been determined, the names are placed in grade order and an eligible list is established. There are various methods for resolving ties between those who get the same final grade – probably the most common is to place first the name of the person whose application was received first. Job offers are made from the eligible list in the order the names appear on it. You will be notified of your grade and your rank as soon as all these computations have been made. This will be done as rapidly as possible.

People who are found to meet the requirements in the announcement are called "eligibles." Their names are put on a list of eligible candidates. An eligible's chances of getting a job depend on how high he stands on this list and how fast agencies are filling jobs from the list.

When a job is to be filled from a list of eligibles, the agency asks for the names of people on the list of eligibles for that job. When the civil service commission receives this request, it sends to the agency the names of the three people highest on this list. Or, if the job to be filled has specialized requirements, the office sends the agency the names of the top three persons who meet these requirements from the general list.

The appointing officer makes a choice from among the three people whose names were sent to him. If the selected person accepts the appointment, the names of the others are put back on the list to be considered for future openings.

That is the rule in hiring from all kinds of eligible lists, whether they are for typist, carpenter, chemist, or something else. For every vacancy, the appointing officer has his choice of any one of the top three eligibles on the list. This explains why the person whose name is on top of the list sometimes does not get an appointment when some of the persons lower on the list do. If the appointing officer chooses the second or third eligible, the No. 1 eligible does not get a job at once, but stays on the list until he is appointed or the list is terminated.

X. HOW TO PASS THE INTERVIEW TEST

The examination for which you applied requires an oral interview test. You have already taken the written test and you are now being called for the interview test – the final part of the formal examination.

You may think that it is not possible to prepare for an interview test and that there are no procedures to follow during an interview. Our purpose is to point out some things you can do in advance that will help you and some good rules to follow and pitfalls to avoid while you are being interviewed.

What is an interview supposed to test?

The written examination is designed to test the technical knowledge and competence of the candidate; the oral is designed to evaluate intangible qualities, not readily measured otherwise, and to establish a list showing the relative fitness of each candidate – as measured against his competitors – for the position sought. Scoring is not on the basis of "right" and "wrong," but on a sliding scale of values ranging from "not passable" to "outstanding." As a matter of fact, it is possible to achieve a relatively low score without a single "incorrect" answer because of evident weakness in the qualities being measured.

Occasionally, an examination may consist entirely of an oral test – either an individual or a group oral. In such cases, information is sought concerning the technical knowledges and abilities of the candidate, since there has been no written examination for this purpose. More commonly, however, an oral test is used to supplement a written examination.

Who conducts interviews?

The composition of oral boards varies among different jurisdictions. In nearly all, a representative of the personnel department serves as chairman. One of the members of the board may be a representative of the department in which the candidate would work. In some cases, "outside experts" are used, and, frequently, a businessman or some other representative of the general public is asked to serve. Labor and management or other special groups may be represented. The aim is to secure the services of experts in the appropriate field.

However the board is composed, it is a good idea (and not at all improper or unethical) to ascertain in advance of the interview who the members are and what groups they represent. When you are introduced to them, you will have some idea of their backgrounds and interests, and at least you will not stutter and stammer over their names.

What should be done before the interview?

While knowledge about the board members is useful and takes some of the surprise element out of the interview, there is other preparation which is more substantive. It *is* possible to prepare for an oral interview – in several ways:

1) Keep a copy of your application and review it carefully before the interview

This may be the only document before the oral board, and the starting point of the interview. Know what education and experience you have listed there, and the sequence and dates of all of it. Sometimes the board will ask you to review the highlights of your experience for them; you should not have to hem and haw doing it.

2) Study the class specification and the examination announcement

Usually, the oral board has one or both of these to guide them. The qualities, characteristics or knowledges required by the position sought are stated in these documents. They offer valuable clues as to the nature of the oral interview. For example, if the job involves supervisory responsibilities, the announcement will usually indicate that knowledge of modern supervisory methods and the qualifications of the candidate as a supervisor will be tested. If so, you can expect such questions, frequently in the form of a hypothetical situation which you are expected to solve. NEVER go into an oral without knowledge of the duties and responsibilities of the job you seek.

3) Think through each qualification required

Try to visualize the kind of questions you would ask if you were a board member. How well could you answer them? Try especially to appraise your own knowledge and background in each area, *measured against the job sought*, and identify any areas in which you are weak. Be critical and realistic – do not flatter yourself.

4) Do some general reading in areas in which you feel you may be weak

For example, if the job involves supervision and your past experience has NOT, some general reading in supervisory methods and practices, particularly in the field of human relations, might be useful. Do NOT study agency procedures or detailed manuals. The oral board will be testing your understanding and capacity, not your memory.

5) Get a good night's sleep and watch your general health and mental attitude

You will want a clear head at the interview. Take care of a cold or any other minor ailment, and of course, no hangovers.

What should be done on the day of the interview?

Now comes the day of the interview itself. Give yourself plenty of time to get there. Plan to arrive somewhat ahead of the scheduled time, particularly if your appointment is in the fore part of the day. If a previous candidate fails to appear, the board might be ready for you a bit early. By early afternoon an oral board is almost invariably behind schedule if there are many candidates, and you may have to wait. Take along a book or magazine to read, or your application to review, but leave any extraneous material in the waiting room when you go in for your interview. In any event, relax and compose yourself.

The matter of dress is important. The board is forming impressions about you – from your experience, your manners, your attitude, and your appearance. Give your personal appearance careful attention. Dress your best, but not your flashiest. Choose conservative, appropriate clothing, and be sure it is immaculate. This is a business interview, and your appearance should indicate that you regard it as such. Besides, being well groomed and properly dressed will help boost your confidence.

Sooner or later, someone will call your name and escort you into the interview room. *This is it*. From here on you are on your own. It is too late for any more preparation. But remember, you asked for this opportunity to prove your fitness, and you are here because your request was granted.

What happens when you go in?

The usual sequence of events will be as follows: The clerk (who is often the board stenographer) will introduce you to the chairman of the oral board, who will introduce you to the other members of the board. Acknowledge the introductions before you sit down. Do not be surprised if you find a microphone facing you or a stenotypist sitting by. Oral interviews are usually recorded in the event of an appeal or other review.

Usually the chairman of the board will open the interview by reviewing the highlights of your education and work experience from your application – primarily for the benefit of the other members of the board, as well as to get the material into the record. Do not interrupt or comment unless there is an error or significant misinterpretation; if that is the case, do not hesitate. But do not quibble about insignificant matters. Also, he will usually ask you some question about your education, experience or your present job – partly to get you to start talking and to establish the interviewing "rapport." He may start the actual questioning, or turn it over to one of the other members. Frequently, each member undertakes the questioning on a particular area, one in which he is perhaps most competent, so you can expect each member to participate in the examination. Because time is limited, you may also expect some rather abrupt switches in the direction the questioning takes, so do not be upset by it. Normally, a board member will not pursue a single line of questioning unless he discovers a particular strength or weakness.

After each member has participated, the chairman will usually ask whether any member has any further questions, then will ask you if you have anything you wish to add. Unless you are expecting this question, it may floor you. Worse, it may start you off on an extended, extemporaneous speech. The board is not usually seeking more information. The question is principally to offer you a last opportunity to present further qualifications or to indicate that you have nothing to add. So, if you feel that a significant qualification or characteristic has been overlooked, it is proper to point it out in a sentence or so. Do not compliment the board on the thoroughness of their examination -- they have been sketchy, and you know it. If you wish, merely say, "No thank you, I have nothing further to add." This is a point where you can "talk yourself out" of a good impression or fail to present an important bit of information. Remember, *you close the interview yourself*.

The chairman will then say, "That is all, Mr. _____, thank you." Do not be startled; the interview is over, and quicker than you think. Thank him, gather your belongings and take your leave. Save your sigh of relief for the other side of the door.

How to put your best foot forward
Throughout this entire process, you may feel that the board individually and collectively is trying to pierce your defenses, seek out your hidden weaknesses and embarrass and confuse you. Actually, this is not true. They are obliged to make an appraisal of your qualifications for the job you are seeking, and they want to see you in your best light. Remember, they must interview all candidates and a non-cooperative candidate may become a failure in spite of their best efforts to bring out his qualifications. Here are 15 suggestions that will help you:

1) Be natural – Keep your attitude confident, not cocky
If you are not confident that you can do the job, do not expect the board to be. Do not apologize for your weaknesses, try to bring out your strong points. The board is interested in a positive, not negative, presentation. Cockiness will antagonize any board member and make him wonder if you are covering up a weakness by a false show of strength.

2) Get comfortable, but don't lounge or sprawl
Sit erectly but not stiffly. A careless posture may lead the board to conclude that you are careless in other things, or at least that you are not impressed by the importance of the occasion. Either conclusion is natural, even if incorrect. Do not fuss with your clothing, a pencil or an ashtray. Your hands may occasionally be useful to emphasize a point; do not let them become a point of distraction.

3) Do not wisecrack or make small talk
This is a serious situation, and your attitude should show that you consider it as such. Further, the time of the board is limited – they do not want to waste it, and neither should you.

4) Do not exaggerate your experience or abilities

In the first place, from information in the application or other interviews and sources, the board may know more about you than you think. Secondly, you probably will not get away with it. An experienced board is rather adept at spotting such a situation, so do not take the chance.

5) If you know a board member, do not make a point of it, yet do not hide it

Certainly you are not fooling him, and probably not the other members of the board. Do not try to take advantage of your acquaintanceship – it will probably do you little good.

6) Do not dominate the interview

Let the board do that. They will give you the clues – do not assume that you have to do all the talking. Realize that the board has a number of questions to ask you, and do not try to take up all the interview time by showing off your extensive knowledge of the answer to the first one.

7) Be attentive

You only have 20 minutes or so, and you should keep your attention at its sharpest throughout. When a member is addressing a problem or question to you, give him your undivided attention. Address your reply principally to him, but do not exclude the other board members.

8) Do not interrupt

A board member may be stating a problem for you to analyze. He will ask you a question when the time comes. Let him state the problem, and wait for the question.

9) Make sure you understand the question

Do not try to answer until you are sure what the question is. If it is not clear, restate it in your own words or ask the board member to clarify it for you. However, do not haggle about minor elements.

10) Reply promptly but not hastily

A common entry on oral board rating sheets is "candidate responded readily," or "candidate hesitated in replies." Respond as promptly and quickly as you can, but do not jump to a hasty, ill-considered answer.

11) Do not be peremptory in your answers

A brief answer is proper – but do not fire your answer back. That is a losing game from your point of view. The board member can probably ask questions much faster than you can answer them.

12) Do not try to create the answer you think the board member wants

He is interested in what kind of mind you have and how it works – not in playing games. Furthermore, he can usually spot this practice and will actually grade you down on it.

13) Do not switch sides in your reply merely to agree with a board member

Frequently, a member will take a contrary position merely to draw you out and to see if you are willing and able to defend your point of view. Do not start a debate, yet do not surrender a good position. If a position is worth taking, it is worth defending.

14) Do not be afraid to admit an error in judgment if you are shown to be wrong

The board knows that you are forced to reply without any opportunity for careful consideration. Your answer may be demonstrably wrong. If so, admit it and get on with the interview.

15) Do not dwell at length on your present job

The opening question may relate to your present assignment. Answer the question but do not go into an extended discussion. You are being examined for a *new* job, not your present one. As a matter of fact, try to phrase ALL your answers in terms of the job for which you are being examined.

Basis of Rating

Probably you will forget most of these "do's" and "don'ts" when you walk into the oral interview room. Even remembering them all will not ensure you a passing grade. Perhaps you did not have the qualifications in the first place. But remembering them will help you to put your best foot forward, without treading on the toes of the board members.

Rumor and popular opinion to the contrary notwithstanding, an oral board wants you to make the best appearance possible. They know you are under pressure – but they also want to see how you respond to it as a guide to what your reaction would be under the pressures of the job you seek. They will be influenced by the degree of poise you display, the personal traits you show and the manner in which you respond.

ABOUT THIS BOOK

This book contains tests divided into Examination Sections. Go through each test, answering every question in the margin. We have also attached a sample answer sheet at the back of the book that can be removed and used. At the end of each test look at the answer key and check your answers. On the ones you got wrong, look at the right answer choice and learn. Do not fill in the answers first. Do not memorize the questions and answers, but understand the answer and principles involved. On your test, the questions will likely be different from the samples. Questions are changed and new ones added. If you understand these past questions you should have success with any changes that arise. Tests may consist of several types of questions. We have additional books on each subject should more study be advisable or necessary for you. Finally, the more you study, the better prepared you will be. This book is intended to be the last thing you study before you walk into the examination room. Prior study of relevant texts is also recommended. NLC publishes some of these in our Fundamental Series. Knowledge and good sense are important factors in passing your exam. Good luck also helps. So now study this Passbook, absorb the material contained within and take that knowledge into the examination. Then do your best to pass that exam.

EXAMINATION SECTION

EXAMINATION SECTION
TEST 1

DIRECTIONS: Each question or incomplete statement is followed by several suggested answers or completions. Select the one that BEST answers the question or completes the statement. *PRINT THE LETTER OF THE CORRECT ANSWER IN THE SPACE AT THE RIGHT.*

1. A nurse instructing a family in the home should emphasize that of the following the MOST effective way of controlling tuberculosis infection is to 1.____

    A. soak all the patient's linen in soap and water solution for 6 hours before laundering
    B. admit no one to the room except the attendant
    C. have the patient cover his mouth and nose with disposable tissues when coughing or expectorating
    D. remove all rugs, curtains, and unnecessary furniture from the room

2. When a post-operative patient complains of pain in the calf of the leg, aggravated by dorsiflexion of the foot, the BEST course of action for the nurse to take is to recommend 2.____

    A. hot soakings
    B. walking about to relieve pain
    C. massaging locally
    D. remaining in bed and calling the doctor

3. Morbidity rates are statistics relative to 3.____

    A. births   B. deaths
    C. sickness and disease   D. marriages

4. The Snellen test is a 4.____

    A. visual screening test   B. diagnostic test for syphilis
    C. blood test for anemia   D. hearing test

5. The nurse should instruct families that the temperature of water for hot water bottles should be between 5.____

    A. 95° and 110° F   B. 115° and 130° F
    C. 135° and 150° F   D. 155° and 170° F

6. When planning a feeding schedule for a premature infant, it is of PRIMARY importance to 6.____

    A. feed the baby regularly every two hours
    B. establish a food tolerance since the intestinal tract is undeveloped
    C. include Vitamins A, B, C, D and K in the feeding
    D. provide for additional carbohydrates

7. B.C.G. vaccine is being given at the present time 7.____

    A. to all children with a positive tuberculin test
    B. to all children exposed to tuberculosis

C. to all children with minimal tuberculosis lesions
D. experimentally to non-reactors to the tuberculin test who are subject to frequent exposure to tuberculosis

8. When teaching a colostomy patient self-care at home, the MOST important point for the nurse to emphasize is that

   A. a colostomy bag is essential to assure safety from leakage
   B. the irrigation can should hang five feet above hip level
   C. the irrigation should be done at the same time each day
   D. the irrigation should be followed by one hour of bed-rest

9. The destruction of all organisms, including spores, is known as

   A. disinfection
   B. sterilization
   C. antiseptic action
   D. germicidal action

10. The MOST frequent and serious complication likely to arise after a patient has undergone surgery is

    A. wound infection
    B. blood poisoning
    C. respiratory infection
    D. decubitus ulcers

11. A disarrangement of the normal relation of the bones entering into the formation of a joint BEST defines

    A. a dislocation
    B. a fracture
    C. a sprain
    D. ankylosis

12. The Non-Protein Nitrogen (N.P.N.) test is a

    A. blood test to determine renal function
    B. blood test to determine liver function
    C. urine test to determine concentration
    D. patency test of the Fallopian tubes

13. When eating pork, a person may AVOID trichinosis by

    A. not eating it in warm weather
    B. soaking it in salt water two hours before cooking
    C. buying pork which has a government inspection stamp
    D. thoroughly cooking it

14. Beriberi is a nutritional disease caused by lack of a sufficient amount of vitamin

    A. A
    B. B_1
    C. B_{12}
    D. K

15. The one of the following groups of foods which is the BEST source of thiamine is

    A. milk, egg yolks, cheese, lettuce
    B. green peas, broccoli, kale, cabbage
    C. escarole, carrots, cream cheese
    D. whole grain bread and cereals, pork, organ meats

16. The vitamin believed to be of GREATEST aid in the healing of wounds is vitamin

    A. B_2 B. B_{12} C. C   D. D

17. Following the ingestion of contaminated food, acute food poisoning USUALLY occurs after the elapse of from _____ hours.

    A. 2 to 6   B. 7 to 12
    C. 13 to 24   D. 25 to 36

18. A slowly progressive degenerative disease of the nervous system usually occurring in or after middle life, and characterized by tremors and rigidity of the skeletal muscles, BEST defines the condition known as

    A. arthritis   B. Parkinson's disease
    C. Jacksonian epilepsy   D. multiple sclerosis

19. Of the following, the PREFERRED site for intramuscular injections is

    A. the deltoid muscle
    B. the quadriceps muscle
    C. any section of the buttocks
    D. the upper outer quadrant of the buttock near its inner angle

20. Of the following, the one which is MALIGNANT is

    A. papilloma   B. lipoma
    C. lymphosarcoma   D. myoma

21. Of the following organisms, the one which causes MORE THAN HALF of all kidney infections is

    A. bacterium coli   B. staphylocoecus
    C. streptococcus   D. escherichia coli

22. Of the following antibiotics, the one which produces a TOXIC effect on the auditory nerve is

    A. chloromycetin   B. aureomycin
    C. streptomycin   D. penicillin

23. Antibiotics are UNIFORMLY excreted through the

    A. skin   B. urine   C. stool   D. lungs

24. Isonicotinic acid hydrazide is used CHIEFLY in the treatment of

    A. rheumatic fever   B. arthritis
    C. cancer   D. tuberculosis

25. The one of the following which attacks the enamel of the teeth is

    A. gingivitis   B. dental caries
    C. pyorrhea alveolaris   D. vitamin C deficiency

KEY (CORRECT ANSWERS)

1. C
2. D
3. C
4. A
5. B

6. B
7. D
8. C
9. D
10. C

11. A
12. A
13. D
14. B
15. D

16. C
17. B
18. B
19. D
20. C

21. A
22. C
23. B
24. D
25. B

———

TEST 2

DIRECTIONS: Each question or incomplete statement is followed by several suggested answers or completions. Select the one that BEST answers the question or completes the statement. *PRINT THE LETTER OF THE CORRECT ANSWER IN THE SPACE AT THE RIGHT.*

1. Failure of muscle coordination to bring the image of an object upon the fovea centralis retinae at the same time in each eye BEST defines the condition known as

   A. glaucoma
   B. optic neuritis
   C. retrobulbar neuritis
   D. strabismus

   1.____

2. ANOTHER term for farsightedness is

   A. hyperopia
   B. myopia
   C. ophthalmia
   D. astigmatism

   2.____

3. A condition which in its advanced stages is characterized by symptoms of halos or rainbows around light is known as

   A. cataracts
   B. detached retina
   C. glaucoma
   D. corneal ulcers

   3.____

4. Blocking of the eustachian tube in children is caused MOST often by

   A. adenoid growth around the nasal end of the tube
   B. deterioration in the inner ear
   C. ear wax
   D. perforation of the eardrum

   4.____

5. It is generally agreed among authorities that a child should have training in lip reading when successive audiometric tests indicate that the better ear shows a LOSS of _____ decibels.

   A. 5
   B. 10
   C. 15
   D. 25

   5.____

6. The MOST satisfactory way to measure a patient for crutches is to have him

   A. stand against a wall, with his arms straight at side
   B. lie on his back, with his arms straight at side
   C. lie on his back, with his arms elevated over his head
   D. stand against a wall, with his arms extended over his head

   6.____

7. In crutch walking, the weight is placed on the

   A. quadriceps muscle
   B. trapezius muscle
   C. deltoid muscle
   D. palms of the hands with wrists in hyperextension

   7.____

8. If a nurse sees that a newborn holds his head to one side with his chin rotated in the opposite direction, she SHOULD recognize the condition as

   A. facial paralysis
   B. cerebral palsy
   C. torticollis
   D. cephalhematoma

   8.____

9. Of the following types of cerebral palsy, the one which is characterized by tense contracted muscles is

   A. spastic
   B. athetoid
   C. ataxic
   D. dystonic

10. Of the following communicable diseases, the one that is characterized by the eruption of successive crops of rose pink spots which change into vesicles and finally into crusts is

    A. chicken pox
    B. German measles
    C. scarlet fever
    D. measles

11. The remarkable reduction in the incidence of typhoid fever is due PRIMARILY to

    A. immunization
    B. control of human environment
    C. the use of antibiotics
    D. isolation of typhoid carriers

12. Antibodies which neutralize toxins are called

    A. lysins
    B. agglutinins
    C. antitoxins
    D. opsonins

13. Brucellosis is USUALLY acquired in man by

    A. direct contact with a human being having the disease
    B. direct contact with infected cattle
    C. ingestion of raw milk or milk products
    D. inhaling bacteria from the air

14. Immunity following successful vaccination against smallpox is now believed to last

    A. for the lifetime of the individual
    B. at least seven years
    C. from one to three years
    D. a varying length of time from individual to individual

15. The gamma globulin fraction of pooled human plasma is an EFFECTIVE agent for preventing or modifying

    A. chicken pox
    B. measles
    C. scarlet fever
    D. diphtheria

16. Of the following, the one which is capable of ALTERING the course of tuberculosis is

    A. streptomycin
    B. B.C.G. vaccine
    C. the tuberculin test
    D. the Schick test

17. Of the following, the FIRST symptom of spontaneous pneumothorax is

    A. tightening of the chest with or without dyspnea
    B. acute dyspnea
    C. anxious expression of the face
    D. restlessness plus anxiety

18. To function effectively in the follow-up of a venereal disease patient, the one MOST important thing for the nurse to know is the

    A. number of contacts the patient has had
    B. correct medical diagnosis of the patient concerned
    C. structure of the family
    D. economic status of the family

19. The incubation period of neisseria gonorrhea is GENERALLY from _____ days.

    A. 3 to 6
    B. 7 to 10
    C. 11 to 14
    D. 15 to 18

20. Of the following, the one which prenatal syphilis SELDOM affects is the

    A. nervous system
    B. spleen
    C. liver
    D. heart

21. Even without treatment, a person infected with non-congenital syphilis is NOT dangerous to others after he has had the disease _____ months.

    A. 6
    B. 12
    C. 18
    D. 2

22. In the treatment of syphilis, the antibiotic which has proven the MOST effective, with the LEAST toxic results, as well as the MOST economical, is

    A. streptomycin
    B. aureomycin
    C. penicillin
    D. chloromycetin

23. Of the following communicable diseases that may be contracted in the first trimester of pregnancy, the one which is BELIEVED to produce malformation in the newborn is

    A. scarlet fever
    B. German measles
    C. diphtheria
    D. measles

24. In the normal course of pregnancy, the total blood volume

    A. decreases
    B. increases and decreases at various times
    C. remains normal
    D. increases

25. In fetal growth, the period characterized by membranous nails and tooth buds occurs at the end of the _____ lunar month.

    A. 1st
    B. 3rd
    C. 5th
    D. 7th

KEY (CORRECT ANSWERS)

1.	D	11.	B
2.	A	12.	C
3.	C	13.	C
4.	A	14.	D
5.	D	15.	B
6.	B	16.	A
7.	D	17.	A
8.	C	18.	B
9.	A	19.	A
10.	A	20.	D

21. D
22. C
23. B
24. D
25. B

TEST 3

DIRECTIONS: Each question or incomplete statement is followed by several suggested answers or completions. Select the one that BEST answers the question or completes the statement. *PRINT THE LETTER OF THE CORRECT ANSWER IN THE SPACE AT THE RIGHT.*

1. The exercises included in the program of "natural childbirth" are PRIMARILY aimed at

    A. making the waiting time more interesting to the patient
    B. assuring the patient of a painless labor period
    C. relaxing the patient
    D. eliminating the use of anesthesia during labor

2. The UNDERLYING principle of "rooming in" for newborn infants and their mothers is that it

    A. prevents nursery infections in the baby
    B. requires less nursing time
    C. provides an opportunity for the mother to know and care for her baby while in the hospital
    D. encourages breast feeding

3. Erythroblastosis due to the RH factor in newborn infants MOST frequently results from

    A. transfusing an RH negative woman with RH positive blood
    B. the mating of an RH positive father and an RH negative mother
    C. the failure to determine the RH status of pregnant women
    D. transfusing the mother during pregnancy

4. A premature baby is BEST defined as an infant who

    A. is less than 9 months in gestation
    B. weighs 6 pounds at birth
    C. was born in the 7th month of gestation
    D. weighs 2500 grams or less at birth

5. Retrolental fibroplasia occurs in

    A. premature infants   B. pre-school children
    C. adolescents   D. old age

6. When advising a mother regarding infant feeding, the nurse should know that MOST pediatricians recommend that

    A. babies be fed when they cry
    B. mothers plan a three or four hour schedule and adhere to it without variation
    C. mothers need not adhere to a strict feeding schedule since each child has an individual feeding pattern which should be used as a guide
    D. infants never be fed more often than once every four hours

7. An average normal infant may FIRST be expected to sit alone at the age of _____ months.

    A. 5   B. 7   C. 9   D. 11

8. Of the following, the GREATEST single cause of infant and neonatal mortality is

   A. accidents
   B. prematurity
   C. congenital malformation
   D. pneumonia

9. Of the following statements relating to epilepsy, the one which is MOST correct is that

   A. epilepsy indicates feeblemindedness
   B. children with epilepsy should be treated as invalids
   C. seizures in about 50% of children with epilepsy can best be controlled with medicines now in use
   D. children with epilepsy should have permanent home teaching

10. The MOST rapid period of biological growth is during the _____ period.

    A. prenatal
    B. pre-adolescent
    C. adolescent
    D. post-adolescent

11. A nurse should advise a mother that bowel training is ORDINARILY successful

    A. at the same time as bladder training
    B. earlier than bladder training
    C. later than bladder training
    D. when the child is four months old

12. When cautioning about carbon monoxide poisoning, the nurse should recommend that the family

    A. keep a fire extinguisher handy at all times
    B. inspect gas, appliances daily
    C. keep a window open at least two inches in any room where there is a gas appliance
    D. do not inspect gas appliances with wet hands

13. In the treatment of severe burns, the FIRST consideration should be given to

    A. dressing the burned area
    B. treating for shock
    C. estimating the extent of the burned area
    D. giving large amounts of fluids

14. The FIRST step recommended in first aid treatment for an animal bite is

    A. cleansing the wound thoroughly with soap under running water
    B. application of any antiseptic solution
    C. application of tincture of iodine
    D. application of tincture of iodine followed by a band-aid

Questions 15-19.

DIRECTIONS: Next to Numbers 15 through 19, write the letter preceding the disease or condition mentioned in Column II which is most closely connected with the test mentioned in Column I, Numbers 15 through 19.

	Column I		Column II	
15.	Aschheim-Zondek	A.	tuberculosis	15.____
16.	Dick	B.	syphilis	16.____
17.	Kline	C.	scarlet fever	17.____
18.	Mantoux	D.	pregnancy	18.____
19.	Papanicolaou	E.	diphtheria	19.____
		F.	diabetes	
		G.	cancer	

Questions 20-25.

DIRECTIONS: Next to Numbers 20 through 25, write the letter preceding the term mentioned in Column II which is most closely connected with the definition given in Column I, Numbers 20 through 25.

	Column I		Column II	
20.	Inflammation of the kidneys	A.	cretinism	20.____
21.	Alzeimer's disease	B.	enuresis	21.____
22.	Involuntary passage of urine	C.	geriatrics	22.____
23.	White blood corpuscle	D.	leucocyte	23.____
24.	A form of idiocy and dwarfism	E.	nephritis	24.____
25.	Lateral curvature of the spine	F.	paraphasia	25.____
		G.	scoliosis	
		H.	silicosis	

KEY (CORRECT ANSWERS)

1. C
2. C
3. B
4. D
5. A

6. C
7. C
8. B
9. C
0. A

11. B
12. C
13. B
14. A
15. D

16. C
17. B
18. A
19. G
20. E

21. C
22. B
23. D
24. A
25. G

TEST 4

DIRECTIONS: Each question or incomplete statement is followed by several suggested answers or completions. Select the one that BEST answers the question or completes the statement. *PRINT THE LETTER OF THE CORRECT ANSWER IN THE SPACE AT THE RIGHT.*

1. The victim of a neck fracture should be transported

    A. face downward on a rigid support
    B. face upward on a rigid support
    C. lying on the left side of a rigid support
    D. sitting upright on a chair

2. Of the following, the PRIMARY cause of acne in adolescents is

    A. too much carbohydrate in the diet
    B. the inability of the fat gland ducts and outlets to allow passage of increased secretions of sebum
    C. lack of vitamin A in the diet
    D. lack of good personal hygiene

3. The nutritional needs of older people differ from those of young adults in that older people require MORE

    A. protein   B. minerals   C. calcium   D. calories

4. Planning for aging should be the responsibility CHIEFLY of

    A. the individual   B. the family
    C. industry   D. the total community

5. Prophylaxis against the diseases of old age is USUALLY directed toward

    A. preventing the onset of a disease
    B. preventing or minimizing the disability disease produces
    C. prohibiting all physical exercise
    D. providing for early retirement

6. Of the following, the MOST accurate statement with regard to the life expectancy of the diabetic today is that

    A. his life span is 1/3 that of the non-diabetic
    B. his life span approximates that of the non-diabetic, provided proper precautions are taken
    C. the diabetic seldom lives beyond age 60 because of complications which shorten life
    D. if diabetes occurs in childhood, the prognosis is good for a normal life span

7. N.P.H. insulin is generally considered the MOST valuable of the different types of insulin because it

    A. has a low protamine content as compared with protamine zinc insulin
    B. reaches its peak in eight hours, thus providing safety for the patient during the night

C. is well-adapted to the mild cases
D. meets the requirements of the greatest number of patients

8. When caring for elderly people with diabetes, it is MOST important for the nurse to

    A. know that all diabetics must have insulin daily
    B. understand their individual personalities and habits
    C. teach them how to do urinalysis and give their own insulin
    D. know that their diets require major adjustments

9. The GREATEST social problem affecting health which has increased in the past few years is

    A. juvenile delinquency
    B. juvenile narcotic addiction
    C. crowding of children in housing projects
    D. migration of industrial workers

10. The MOST important reason for the nurse to keep records of patients is to

    A. provide better service to the patients
    B. give information to other agencies in the community
    C. compile information for legal documents
    D. keep *data* for tabulating vital statistics

11. The function of the nurse on a school health council is to

    A. act in an advisory capacity to the principal and teaching staff in matters pertaining to health
    B. secure needed facilities for treatment of children with defects
    C. plan the health education program for the school
    D. organize the entire facilities of the school for the promotion of health

12. With regard to health services, the recommendation for enactment into law that was carried out was that

    A. the Children's Bureau be abolished
    B. compulsory health insurance be inaugurated for all people in the United States
    C. the Federal Security Agency be reorganized into a Department of Health, Education and Welfare
    D. the Children's Bureau and the United States Health Service be combined

13. If a nurse has been assigned the following four visits, all within a radius of a few blocks, she should visit FIRST the case in which a(n)

    A. anxious prenatal patient is going to be evicted from her home
    B. school child was sent home from school because of Koplik spots
    C. newborn baby is regurgitating every other feeding
    D. newborn baby was discharged against the advice of the hospital to a home in which the father has a positive sputum for tuberculosis

14. A nurse is assigned four visits. Of the following, the FIRST visit she should make is to a   14._____

    A. cardiac patient who receives mercuhydrin regularly twice a week
    B. patient receiving 20U. of N.P.H. insulin
    C. mother delivered of a baby by a non-nurse midwife at 4 A.M. that morning
    D. child sent home from school the previous day with a rash resembling scarlet fever

15. Assume that a mother expresses concern over her one-year-old baby's feeding habits.   15._____
    As a nurse, you can BEST advise this mother by telling her that

    A. she should feed her baby, although he refuses to eat
    B. appetites of children begin to diminish at the end of the first year and continue to be small for a year or two
    C. poor eating habits in children are often a result of emotional problems between parents
    D. she should feed her child every two hours whether he is hungry or not

16. Assume that a nine-year-old boy comes to you for help. He has a splinter in his finger   16._____
    which has been embedded for 24 hours and around which there is a reddened *area*.
    The BEST course of action for you to take is to

    A. remove the splinter and apply an antiseptic solution
    B. wash the area with tincture of green soap, express gently, and apply an antiseptic solution
    C. have the boy soak his finger in hot water and instruct him to have his mother continue the soakings at home in order to loosen the splinter
    D. cover the area with a sterile dressing and call the mother to instruct her to take the child to a physician for treatment

17. A city of 100,000 reported 30 maternal deaths last year. Of the following, the statement   17._____
    regarding the maternal death rate which is CORRECT is that it

    A. is 30%
    B. cannot be computed because we do not know the general death rate
    C. cannot be computed because we do not know the number of live births
    D. cannot be computed because we do not know the infant death rate

18. The agency which has as its objective "the attainment of the highest possible level of   18._____
    health of all the people" is the

    A. American Red Cross
    B. World Health Organization
    C. United States Public Health Service
    D. The Children's Bureau

19. In the event of an atom bomb attack, civil defense authorities state that the one of the fol-   19._____
    lowing which will cause the GREATEST number of deaths is

    A. radioactivity   B. injuries
    C. infections   D. hemorrhage

20. Insulin was isolated from other products of the pancreas by   20._____

    A. Louis Pasteur   B. Frederick Banting
    C. George Baker   D. Anton Von Leeuwenhoek

21. Recent studies indicate that the MOST economical and practical public health control method for dental caries is to   21.____

    A. promote a community-wide nutrition program
    B. provide community dental services for bi-yearly examination of school children
    C. provide individual daily fluoride supplements
    D. fluoridate the domestic water supply

22. During a poliomyelitis epidemic, of the following, the one precaution NOT recommended by the National Foundation for Infantile Paralysis is to   22.____

    A. keep clean
    B. avoid new groups
    C. avoid getting chilled
    D. keep children home from school

23. The LEADING cause of all deaths in the United States is   23.____

    A. cancer
    C. accidents
    B. diseases of infancy
    D. heart disease

24. The LEADING cause of school absences in the United States is   24.____

    A. accidents
    C. digestive disorders
    B. skin diseases
    D. respiratory infections

25. The National Cancer Institute established in the U.S. Public Health Service in 1937 has as its MAJOR goal   25.____

    A. research and dissemination of knowledge concerning the causes and treatment of cancer
    B. improving standards for the care of the cancer patient in both the home and hospital
    C. training of medical personnel in the treatment of cancer
    D. granting financial aid to states in the development of cancer control programs

KEY (CORRECT ANSWERS)

1.	B	11.	A
2.	B	12.	C
3.	C	13.	D
4.	D	14.	C
5.	B	15.	B
6.	B	16.	D
7.	D	17.	C
8.	B	18.	B
9.	B	19.	A
10.	A	20.	B

21. D
22. D
23. D
24. D
25. D

EXAMINATION SECTION
TEST 1

DIRECTIONS: Each question or incomplete statement is followed by several suggested answers or completions. Select the one that BEST answers the question or completes the statement. *PRINT THE LETTER OF THE CORRECT ANSWER IN THE SPACE AT THE RIGHT.*

1. A nurse arrives in a home immediately after the birth of a premature baby for whom no preparation has been made. The MOST important factor to be considered in the immediate care of the baby is

   A. maintenance of body temperature
   B. removal to a hospital
   C. feeding with breastmilk
   D. demonstration of the infant's bath to the mother
   E. securing someone to give full-time care to the baby

1.____

2. The CHIEF cause of infant mortality is

   A. gastroenteritis   B. pneumonia
   C. prematurity   D. suffocation
   E. birth injuries

2.____

3. A child who carries the RH positive factor when his mother is an RH negative may develop a condition known as

   A. hypopituitarism   B. erythroblastosis
   C. autosomal genes   D. mongolism
   E. acromegaly

3.____

4. According to studies of child development, the one of the following behavior characteristics which you would expect to find in a normal two-year-old child is

   A. bladder control day and night
   B. ability to play well with a group
   C. ability to feed himself without help
   D. ability to converse in sentences
   E. ability to ride a tricycle

4.____

5. Authorities are agreed that the BEST time to begin training a child for bladder control is

   A. as soon as the mother observes a definite rhythm in urination
   B. when the child begins to walk
   C. not until the child can indicate verbally a desire to void
   D. at one year of age
   E. at nine months of age

5.____

6. In the age group 15 to 30, the one of the following diseases which is the CHIEF cause of death is

   A. puerperal sepsis   B. heart disease
   C. tuberculosis   D. syphilis
   E. appendicitis

6.____

7. In the age group 55 to 64, the one of the following diseases which is the CHIEF cause of death is

   A. circulatory disease
   B. pneumonia
   C. tuberculosis
   D. hemiplegia
   E. cancer

8. In 1976, the expectancy of life at birth had increased to about 61.5. This was a 20-year saving since 1900.
   Of the following factors, the one to which MOST of this saving in life has been attributed is the

   A. improved living conditions, as a result of higher incomes
   B. effects of the discovery of bacteria
   C. increase in recreational facilities which has lowered nervous tension
   D. curtailment of arduous physical labor due to mechanical inventions
   E. federal, state, and municipal assistance to the indigent and the handicapped

9. The term *acquired immunity,* when used in connection with communicable disease, means the

   A. specific immunity developed as a result of a natural selection in a group of people living in any particular area
   B. immunity existing in an area where people have never contracted the disease
   C. immunity existing for a few months after birth given physiologically to the newborn baby by the mother
   D. specific immunity resulting from an attack of the disease or from artificial means
   E. immunity human beings have against certain diseases of lower animals

10. Children who have had rheumatic fever and, as a result, exhibit symptoms of heart disease, must be given special protection against

    A. exposure to acute communicable diseases
    B. cathartics which contain kidney irritants
    C. dietary fads to control weight
    D. sight and sounds which frighten them
    E. living in an enervating warm climate

11. A twenty-one-year-old man is found by x-ray to have minimal tuberculosis. The physician orders sanitorium care. Temporarily no beds are available.
    The BEST advice the nurse can give in this instance until he can be admitted to the sanitorium is to

    A. encourage the man to visit a friend in Arizona.
    B. plan bed rest and isolation of the patient at home where his mother can care for him
    C. advise that he may continue work in his office position since the work is light and the lesion minimal
    D. encourage a seashore vacation where he may lie for hours in the sun
    E. advise an outdoor mountain vacation

12. The time of a well-prepared nurse in a busy syphilis clinic can BEST be used in

A. acting as receptionist to put patients at ease
B. giving intravenous treatments, thereby releasing the physicians to do physical examinations
C. taking histories and interpreting the disease and its treatment to patients
D. assisting the physician and taking notes on his physical examinations
E. managing the clinic smoothly so patients need not wait

13. The effect of syphilitic involvement of the eighth nerve in individuals with congenital syphilis is that it

    A. usually causes facial paralysis, if the patient is not treated promptly
    B. manifests itself very slowly and, therefore, may be easily controlled
    C. is a relatively unimportant complication of the disease and responds readily to treatment
    D. may be disregarded as a probable complication of the disease if the patient is over 6 years old
    E. usually causes total deafness and is not readily responsive to treatment

14. The only way in which syphilis can be detected with CERTAINTY in pregnant women is by

    A. actual discovery of active lesions, since in a new case the serology will remain negative until after parturition
    B. a vaginal smear and dark-field examination, since in pregnancy the spirochetes migrate to the vagina mucosa
    C. a careful case history, since recent discoveries indicate that serologic tests are non-specific in pregnancy
    D. routine serologic tests, since the primary and secondary signs and symptoms are often repressed in pregnancy
    E. the Rorschach test

15. The method which is GENERALLY recommended for preventing premature infant deaths resulting from inter-cranial hemorrhage is to

    A. administer vitamin K to the mother before delivery and to the baby after birth
    B. give the mother massive doses of calcium by hypodermic injection
    C. increase the amount of codliver oil given to the mother so that the calcium is better utilized by the baby
    D. give the infant parathyroid hormone in order to utilize available calcium
    E. give the baby transfusions of gum tragacanth in normal saline

16. The MOST important factor in the control of breast cancer is

    A. application of radium as soon as a lump appears in the breast
    B. deep x-ray therapy of all suspected lipomas
    C. biopsy of the glands in the axilla
    D. operative intervention early in the disease
    E. breastfeeding of infants as a preventive measure

17. Although there are still many unknown factors in the complete etiology of cancer, there is one to which authorities agree cancer can usually be validly attributed.
    This factor is

A. the tendency to cancerous growths passed on in the chromosomes and genes
B. the mechanical action of finely divided airborne proteins
C. chronic irritation in various forms
D. degeneration of cells in the older age groups
E. the implantation, in some way yet unknown, of malignant growths

18. The type of tuberculosis that has been generalized as a result of the bacilli having been seeded into the bloodstream from a tuberculosis infection is

    A. miliary tuberculosis
    B. tuberculosis meningitis
    C. tuberculosis enteritis
    D. silicotic tuberculosis
    E. tuberculosis scrofula

19. The MOST common immediate cause of unsuccessful collapse of the lung by artificial pneumothorax is

    A. hemoptysis
    B. cavitation
    C. pleurisy with effusion
    D. caseous lesion
    E. pleural adhesions

20. A child is given the Mantoux test to detect the existence of tuberculosis infection. After three days, a raised edematous reddened area appears at the site of the test.
    The CORRECT interpretation of the test result is:

    A. A primary infection is present which makes the child completely resistant to further exogenous infections
    B. The test shows evidence of infection, but does not indicate whether the process is active or quiescent
    C. The test shows evidence of active pulmonary tuberculosis
    D. The reaction may be due to protein sensitivity and a control test is required to eliminate this factor
    E. The child has been exposed to active tuberculosis, but has not acquired an infection

21. Of the following, the one which should receive the MOST emphasis by the school nurse in order to achieve the best results in improving school health education is

    A. classroom teaching in hygiene
    B. home visits to expand parent education
    C. assisting teachers to integrate health education in classroom teaching
    D. active participation in the health education programs of Parent-Teacher Associations
    E. parent education through group instruction at the time of the school health examination

22. A high school student is found to have a heart condition which warrants bed rest at home. Because only six weeks of the school term remain, the student wishes to complete the term, and is inclined to disregard the school physician's advice until the school term closes.
    The BEST method the school nurse can take in handling this situation is to

A. visit the home to enlist the parents' cooperation and assist them in planning the necessary care, and encourage the student to follow the doctor's advice
B. discuss it with the school doctor and get his suggestions for adjustment in the school schedule to allow the student to complete the school term
C. refer the student to the Visiting Nurse Association for follow-up and instruction
D. advise the student that if she does remain in school to go to bed every day as soon as she gets home from school
E. advise the student to see her pharmacist for confirmation of the school physician's diagnosis

23. The one of the following criteria which is the BEST method for evaluating the success of the school health program is

    A. improved health behavior as evidenced by the application of health knowledge in daily habits of living
    B. an increased number of health classes in the school curriculum
    C. the number of defects discovered and corrected in school children
    D. the number of school children examined annually by their family physicians
    E. an increased number of children entering school each year without defects

24. A kindgergarten school child is found by a visual acuity test to have 20/30 vision. The action the school nurse should take in this situation is to

    A. send the child to an oculist for a complete eye examination
    B. send a note to the child's parents advising that the child should wear glasses
    C. do nothing since farsightedness is normal in young children
    D. advise the teacher to reduce the amount of class work required of the child until the condition is corrected
    E. enlist the cooperation of parents and teacher in teaching the child good eye hygiene

25. A nurse should know that blepharitis is a(n)

    A. skin disease which is highly communicable
    B. infection of the bladder
    C. inflammation of the eyelids
    D. disease caused by a fungus
    E. nutritional deficiency disease

KEY (CORRECT ANSWERS)

1.	A	11.	B
2.	C	12.	C
3.	B	13.	E
4.	C	14.	D
5.	A	15.	A
6.	C	16.	D
7.	A	17.	C
8.	B	18.	A
9.	D	19.	E
10.	A	20.	B

21. C
22. A
23. A
24. E
25. C

EXAMINATION SECTION
TEST 1

DIRECTIONS: Each question or incomplete statement is followed by several suggested answers or completions. Select the one that BEST answers the question or completes the statement. *PRINT THE LETTER OF THE CORRECT ANSWER IN THE SPACE AT THE RIGHT.*

Questions 1-4.

DIRECTIONS: Questions 1 through 4 are to be answered on the basis of the following information.

A 45-year-old patient is admitted with a severe frontal headache. After a thorough examination, meningitis is ruled out. A CT scan of the head shows multiple ring enhancing lesions. His CO_4 count is 54, and western blot test is positive for HIV.

1. The MOST likely diagnosis of this condition is

    A. cytomegalovirus
    B. mycobacterium aviam intracellulare
    C. histoplasmosis
    D. toxoplasmosis

2. The nurse should do all of the following to protect herself from AIDS infection EXCEPT

    A. exercise care when handling sharp instruments
    B. use disposable mouthpieces and airways instead of direct mouth to mouth resuscitation
    C. wash gloves before use with another patient
    D. wash hands after removing gloves and between patient contact

3. To improve the nutritional status of the patient, all of the following measures should be adopted EXCEPT

    A. including patient in decision-making process regarding his nutritional care
    B. try to give drugs before meals
    C. encourage patient to maximize nutritional intake during periods when he is feeling better
    D. discourage excessive alcohol intake, which has an immunosuppressive effect

4. Nursing interventions facilitating patient understanding of the goals of therapy and methods to prevent HIV transmission include

    A. encouraging patient to discuss feelings and concerns about the plan of therapy and changes in work, home, and lifestyle environment
    B. using a nonjudgmental approach during care
    C. warning patient not to share toilet articles or donate blood or organs
    D. all of the above

Questions 5-8.

DIRECTIONS: Questions 5 through 8 are to be answered on the basis of the following information.

A 29-year-old black male has a cough with mucopurulent sputum, hemoptysis, and dyspnea, with a history of low-grade fever, night sweats, and weight loss. His laboratory workup confirms the diagnosis of pulmonary tuberculosis.

5. Risk factors for the activation of tuberculosis include all of the following EXCEPT

   A. close contact with someone who has infectious tuberculosis
   B. infection with a sexually transmitted disease
   C. a tuberculin skin test which has recently converted to a significant reaction
   D. declining immunity or infection with HIV

6. Nursing education of this patient would NOT include

   A. techniques to control propagation of secretions while coughing
   B. stressing the need to breathe only filtered, humidified air
   C. stressing the importance of a nutritious diet
   D. all of the above

7. In a preventive treatment plan for tuberculosis, isoniazid prophylaxis should be offered to all of the following EXCEPT

   A. household members and other close associates of potentially infectious tuberculous cases
   B. persons recently testing negative to tuberculin reaction
   C. newly infected persons
   D. persons with past tuberculosis

8. Complications of isoniazid therapy that a nurse should have in mind when initiating prophylaxis include all of the following EXCEPT

   A. persistent paresthesias of the hands and feet
   B. progressive liver damage
   C. loss of appetite, fatigue, joint pain, and dark urine
   D. bone marrow suppression

9. Nursing guidelines for the prevention of salmonella infections do NOT include

   A. washing hands after using the toilet, particularly during illness and carrier states
   B. raw eggs or egg drinks should not be ingested
   C. purchase only kosher meats and meat products
   D. all food from animal sources should be thoroughly cooked

10. After eating lunch in a roadside restaurant, a patient develops fever, crampy abdominal pain, diarrhea, mixed blood and mucus, and profound prostration.
    Nursing interventions in the management of this disorder include all of the following EXCEPT

    A. assessing patient for dehydration
    B. offering a caffeinated liquid during acute stage of illness
    C. assisting in epidemiological study of every patient in whom organism is found
    D. instructing patient to avoid taking antimotility agents

11. Measures which should be taken in the prevention of this disorder do NOT include 11._____

    A. prophylactic vaccination of all children under 12 years of age
    B. a program of fly control
    C. surveillance of water sanitation
    D. an adequate sewage disposal program

Questions 12-13.

DIRECTIONS: Questions 12 and 13 are to be answered on the basis of the following information.

After drinking water from a restaurant, a 25-year-old man develops fever, headache, malaise, a non-productive cough, and irregularly spaced small rose-colored spots on his abdomen, chest, and back. His pulse is relatively slow in comparison with his fever.

12. All of the following complications may be expected in this patient EXCEPT 12._____

    A. intestinal hemorrhage and perforation
    B. thrombophelibitis
    C. multiple sclerosis
    D. osteomyelitis

13. Environmental hygiene should be established to prevent enteric fever in endemic areas by 13._____

    A. avoiding all fresh fruits and vegetables
    B. homogenization of all milk and dairy products
    C. protection and purification of water supplies
    D. all of the above

Questions 14-16.

DIRECTIONS: Questions 14 through 16 are to be answered on the basis of the following information.

Two days after a 29-year-old male was hit by a car, he develops headache, fever, and becomes hyperirritable and restless, with rigidity of both flexor and extensor muscles. After a thorough laboratory investigation, he is diagnosed with a case of tetanus.

14. Complications that may be expected in this patient include all of the following EXCEPT 14._____

    A. dysrhythmias   B. cerebrovascular accident
    C. cardiac arrest   D. bacterial shock

15. Nursing interventions in preventing respiratory and cardiovascular complications include all of the following EXCEPT 15._____

    A. monitoring for dysphagia
    B. providing cardiac monitoring
    C. delaying intubation and mechanical ventilation as long as possible if spasms are interfering with respiratory function
    D. maintaining an adequate airway

16. Nursing interventions in the ongoing assessment and support of this patient include

    A. placing the patient in a completely dark, soundproof environment to avoid stimulating reflex spasms
    B. watching for excessive urinary output
    C. avoiding sudden stimuli and light as the slightest stimulation may trigger paroxysmal spasms
    D. all of the above

17. Lyme disease is caused by borrelia burgdorferi and is introduced by an ixodid tick. Nursing instructions for people living in or visiting an endemic area would NOT include

    A. applying insect repellent
    B. tucking pants into boots or socks
    C. removing tick with forceps, exerting slow, steady upward pull, and avoid squeezing the tick
    D. cut a shallow X across the tick bite with a sterile blade

18. Nursing interventions to make patients aware of sexual practices that will reduce the chances of acquiring a sexually transmitted disease include all of the following EXCEPT

    A. avoiding sex with individuals who have had multiple partners
    B. not using water-soluble lubricants
    C. avoiding douching before and after sex
    D. use latex condoms lubricated with nonoxynol-9

19. Diseases that are NOT transmitted via respiratory secretions include

    A. tuberculosis
    B. AIDS
    C. rubeola
    D. rheumatic fever

20. Diseases transmitted via blood and body fluids do NOT include

    A. AIDS
    B. hepatitis B
    C. hepatitis A
    D. all of the above

21. Patients at high risk for social isolation include those infected with

    A. tetanus
    B. tuberculosis
    C. AIDS
    D. all of the above

22. All of the following conditions are prevalent in advanced age EXCEPT

    A. osteoporosis
    B. scoliosis
    C. cataracts
    D. multiple sclerosis

23. Impaired physical mobility related to muscular weakness may be found in patients with

    A. Parkinson's disease
    B. rheumatoid arthritis
    C. cerebral palsy
    D. all of the above

24. Nursing interventions to assist patients in coping with their health problems do NOT include   24._____

    A. referral to support groups
    B. understanding and patience
    C. referral for psychoanalysis
    D. none of the above

25. Patients with, conditions that may be expected to degenerate include those with   25._____

    A. cerebrovascular accidents
    B. multiple sclerosis
    C. spinal cord injuries
    D. all of the above

KEY (CORRECT ANSWERS)

1.	D	11.	A
2.	C	12.	C
3.	B	13.	C
4.	D	14.	B
5.	B	15.	C
6.	B	16.	C
7.	B	17.	D
8.	D	18.	B
9.	C	19.	B
10.	B	20.	C

21. D
22. D
23. A
24. C
25. B

TEST 2

DIRECTIONS: Each question or incomplete statement is followed by several suggested answers or completions. Select the one that BEST answers the question or completes the statement. *PRINT THE LETTER OF THE CORRECT ANSWER IN THE SPACE AT THE RIGHT.*

Questions 1-6.

DIRECTIONS: Questions 1 through 6 are to be answered on the basis of the following information.

A 29-year-old white male has a closed, oblique fracture of the tibia and fibula resulting from a traffic accident.

1. Nursing interventions in the management of this patient involve all of the following EXCEPT

    A. relieving pain and discomfort
    B. promoting complete physical immobilization
    C. preventing the development of disuse syndrome
    D. promoting a positive psychological response to trauma

    1.____

2. In the above patient, a closed reduction is done and a cast is applied. Nursing interventions to dry a plaster cast properly include all of the following EXCEPT

    A. avoid handling cast when wet, if possible; handle with palms, not fingertips
    B. avoid placing the cast on a hard surface while drying
    C. use a heat lamp or hair dryer to speed drying time
    D. not to completely cover the cast

    2.____

3. Nursing care of the patient to maintain good circulation after the cast is applied does NOT include

    A. observing for the five P's (pain, pallor, paralysis, paresthesia, and pulselessness) of neurovascular assessment for muscle ischemia
    B. observing circulatory status in exposed fingers or toes
    C. cutting out pressure areas of the cast on the extremity
    D. all of the above

    3.____

4. In this type of fracture, complications associated with immobility include all of the following EXCEPT

    A. loss of muscle strength and endurance
    B. loss of range of motion/joint contracture
    C. pressure sores at bony prominences
    D. muscular hypertrophy

    4.____

5. Nursing interventions to aid in preventing development of thromboembolism include

    A. encourage immobility, do not change position frequently, and discourage ambulation
    B. elevate legs to prevent statis, avoiding pressure on blood vessels

    5.____

C. avoid elastic stockings or sequential compression devices
D. all of the above

6. In setting the discharge plan, the nurse should advise the patient to

   A. adjust usual lifestyle and responsibilities to accommodate limitations imposed by fracture
   B. start active exercises and continue with isometric exercises after the cast is removed
   C. carefully limit the amount of weight bearing that will be permitted on the fractured extremity
   D. all of the above

Questions 7-9.

DIRECTIONS: Questions 7 through 9 are to be answered on the basis of the following information.

A 65-year-old female suffers a fracture of the right hip joint after slipping on a wet floor. After thorough evaluation of the case, a total hip replacement is performed.

7. Nursing interventions in promoting the comfort of the patient include all of the following EXCEPT

   A. placing a pillow on the outer sides of both the legs to keep affected leg in adduction
   B. with two nurses positioned on each side of the bed, using the draw sheet to lift and reposition the patient in bed
   C. placing the patient in a supine position, placing a pillow under the affected leg from mid-thigh to ankle, keeping the leg in a neutral rotation
   D. handling the affected extremity gently

8. All of the following complications may be suspected in this patient EXCEPT

   A. pneumonia   B. cardiac arrest
   C. fat emboli   D. infection

9. In discussing the discharge plan with the patient and her family, the nurse should recommend all of the following precautions EXCEPT:

   A. Do not lift heavy objects
   B. Do not cross or twist legs
   C. Observe carefully for signs of wound infection
   D. Try to sleep on operative side

10. A 20-year-old male has a suspected fracture of the lumbar spine.
    Nursing interventions to avoid complications associated with spinal fracture and immobility do NOT include

    A. measures to prevent risk of thromboembolism complications
    B. monitoring bowel and bladder function
    C. encouraging the patient to ambulate as soon as possible
    D. all of the above

11. Traction is the force applied in a specific direction. Purposes of traction include all of the following EXCEPT

    A. reduction and immobilization of the fracture
    B. increasing muscle spasms
    C. regaining normal length and alignment of an injured extremity
    D. preventing deformity

12. Nursing interventions in the care of a patient on traction do NOT include

    A. encouraging deep breathing hourly to facilitate expansion of lungs and movement of respiratory secretions
    B. encouraging active exercise of uninvolved muscles
    C. adding progressively heavier weights to the traction apparatus
    D. that the traction must be continuous to be effective

13. Total hip replacement is indicated in all of the following clinical conditions EXCEPT

    A. complete dislocation of the hip joint
    B. pathological fractures from metastatic cancer
    C. femoral neck fracture
    D. congenital hip disease

14. A 26-year-old male has an above knee amputation performed after severe traumatic injury.
    Nursing intervention in the education of this patient includes teaching

    A. the patient and his family how to wrap the residual limb with elastic bandage to control edema and to form a firm conical shape for prosthesis fitting
    B. the patient residual limb-conditioning by pushing the residual limb against a soft pillow
    C. methods of care of the residual limb and prosthesis, washing and drying the limb thoroughly at least twice a day, and removing all soap residue to prevent skin irritation or infection
    D. all of the above

15. A patient with multiple myeloma is admitted to the hospital.
    Nursing interventions to prevent pathological fractures include

    A. assisting the patient in movement with gentleness and patience
    B. allowing the joints to bend freely when repositioning the patient
    C. keeping the patient immobile
    D. all of the above

16. A 58-year-old nulliparous white female is admitted for alcohol detoxification. In the assessment of this patient, the nurse notes that she is at high risk for osteoporosis.
    The nurse should advise the patient all of the following EXCEPT

    A. dietary supplements to minimize bone mass
    B. participating in dietary education related to vitamin D intake
    C. vigorous exercise
    D. strategies to prevent falls

17. A 38-year-old patient is admitted for rheumatoid arthritis. 17.____
    Nursing interventions to aid the patient in adjusting to the chronic nature of this condition include all of the following EXCEPT

    A. advising that continuous immobilization may decrease pain
    B. allowing the patient to express fears and concerns
    C. encouraging continued follow-up to re-evaluate progression of disease and efficacy of drug therapy
    D. teaching the patient to avoid sudden jarring movements of joints

18. Predisposing factors for a herniated lumbar disk include all of the following EXCEPT 18.____

    A. sedentary occupations
    B. frequent physical exercise
    C. long-term driving, e.g., truckdriver
    D. participation in bowling or baseball

19. Nursing interventions to keep a patient with a herniated lumbar disk free of pain include 19.____

    A. bed rest on a firm mattress with bed board; traction as ordered
    B. administering morphine every 6-8 hours
    C. encouraging an exercise program of trunk-twists and deep knee bends
    D. all of the above

20. Indications for surgical intervention in patients with herniated lumbar disks include all of the following EXCEPT 20.____

    A. prevention of further nerve damage and deficits
    B. intermittent back and leg pain
    C. sensory and motor deficits in lower extremities
    D. bowel and bladder dysfunction

Questions 21-23.

DIRECTIONS: Questions 21 through 23 are to be answered on the basis of the following information.

A 25-year-old male sustains an acute head injury after a traffic accident.

21. Nursing interventions for the detection of CSF or blood draining from the nose or ears include all of the following EXCEPT 21.____

    A. observe and record, at least hourly, any leak of blood or clear fluid from the nose or ears
    B. pack nose or ears
    C. immediately report to physician if any drainage is found
    D. drain fluid onto sterile towels or dressings

22. Nursing interventions to keep the patient free from infection or injury include 22.____

    A. seizure precautions
    B. strict aseptic techniques during all invasive procedures
    C. restricting visitors with any respiratory illness
    D. all of the above

23. The patient is undergoing intracranial surgery.
    Nursing interventions to prevent post-operative complications include all of the following EXCEPT

    A. checking ears, nose, and dressings for drainage
    B. suctioning through the nose
    C. supporting head when turning the patient
    D. monitoring breathing, advising the patient that he must not cough

24. A 75-year-old woman is admitted with CVA caused by hemorrhage.
    Nursing interventions in the care of this patient include all of the following EXCEPT

    A. elevating head of the bed 30-45° to improve venous drainage
    B. decreasing environmental stimuli
    C. turning patient gently to the affected side
    D. maintaining complete bedrest until bleeding has been controlled and patient's condition is stable

25. In a patient with Parkinson's disease, nursing interventions to help maintain gastrointestinal integrity include all of the following EXCEPT

    A. providing adequate fluid intake
    B. restricting carbohydrates
    C. providing a high-fiber diet
    D. administering stool softeners or laxatives as ordered

26. Nursing interventions to maintain positive body image and self-concept would NOT include

    A. providing clothes that are simple to put on
    B. supervising and assisting in skin care and personal hygiene
    C. installing a mirror that can easily be seen by the patient
    D. all of the above

27. Myasthenia gravis is diagnosed in a 45-year-old white female.
    Nursing interventions to keep the patient free from respiratory impairment include which of the following?

    A. Postural drainage; turning patient frequently
    B. Diaphragmatic breathing exercises to maintain strength with maximum ventilation and minimum energy expenditure
    C. Balancing physical activities with rest
    D. All of the above

28. Nursing care to keep the patient mentioned above well-nourished would NOT include

    A. providing small, frequent, semisolid or fluid meals that are nutritious and high in potassium
    B. inserting a feeding tube
    C. observing for aspiration; keeping suction equipment available
    D. allowing patient to eat meals without rushing

Questions 29-30.

DIRECTIONS: Questions 29 and 30 are to be answered on the basis of the following information.

A 30-year-old white female develops nystagmus, intentional tremors, and spastic weakness of limbs. She also has a history of sudden falls while standing, dropping things out of her hands, and urinary incontinence. After a thorough diagnostic work-up, she is diagnosed with multiple sclerosis.

29. Nursing interventions in this case do NOT include   29._____

   A. encouraging optimal activity level
   B. promoting adequate rest periods to prevent exhaustion
   C. providing self-help devices for eating, ambulation, and reading
   D. restraining patient while in bed

30. Nursing interventions to make the patient clearly under stand and express her fears do NOT include   30._____

   A. talking to the patient and family together and separately
   B. encouraging patient to begin psychotherapy treatment
   C. allowing expression of depression and hopelessness
   D. clarifying misconceptions and lack of information about present status and prognosis

KEY (CORRECT ANSWERS)

1. B		11. B	
2. C		12. C	
3. C		13. A	
4. D		14. D	
5. B		15. A	
6. D		16. A	
7. A		17. A	
8. B		18. B	
9. D		19. A	
10. C		20. B	
21. B		26. C	
22. D		27. D	
23. B		28. B	
24. C		29. D	
25. B		30. B	

EXAMINATION SECTION
TEST 1

DIRECTIONS: Each question or incomplete statement is followed by several suggested answers or completions. Select the one that BEST answers the question or completes the statement. *PRINT THE LETTER OF THE CORRECT ANSWER IN THE SPACE AT THE RIGHT.*

1. The MOST common cause of death before age 65 is

    A. cerebrovascular disease
    B. malignant neoplasm
    C. heart disease
    D. diabetes mellitus
    E. liver cirrhosis

    1.____

2. Of the following, the disease NOT transmitted by mosquitoes is

    A. dengue fever
    B. lymphocytic choriomeningitis
    C. western equine encephalitis
    D. St. Louis encephalitis
    E. yellow fever

    2.____

3. The single MOST effective measure to prevent hookworm infection is

    A. washing hands
    B. washing clothes daily
    C. cooking food at high temperatures
    D. wearing shoes
    E. none of the above

    3.____

4. Transmission of tuberculosis in the United States occurs MOST often by

    A. fomites
    B. blood transfusion
    C. inhalation of droplet
    D. transplacentally
    E. milk

    4.____

5. The second MOST common cause of death in the United States is

    A. accident
    B. cancer
    C. cerebrovascular disease
    D. heart disease
    E. AIDS

    5.____

6. All of the following bacteria are spread through fecal-oral transmission EXCEPT

    A. haemophilus influenza type B
    B. campylobacter
    C. escherichia coli
    D. salmonella
    E. shigella

    6.____

7. Routine immunization is particularly important for children in day care because pre-school-aged children currently have the highest age specific incidence of all of the following EXCEPT

    A. H-influenzae type B
    B. neisseria meningitis
    C. measles
    D. rubella
    E. pertussis

    7.____

37

8. Hand washing and masks are necessary for physical contact with all of the following patients EXCEPT

   A. lassa fever
   B. diphtheria
   C. coxsackie virus disease
   D. varicella
   E. plaque

9. Control measures for prevention of tick-borne infections include all of the following EXCEPT:

   A. Tick-infested area should be avoided whenever possible.
   B. If a tick-infested area is entered, protective clothing that covers the arms, legs, and other exposed area should be worn.
   C. Tick/insect repellent should be applied to the skin.
   D. Ticks should be removed promptly.
   E. Daily inspection of pets and removal of ticks is not indicated.

10. The PRINCIPAL reservoir of giardia lamblia infection is

    A. humans
    B. mosquitoes
    C. rodents
    D. sandflies
    E. cats

11. Most community-wide epidemics of giardia lamblia infection result from

    A. inhalation of droplets
    B. eating infected meats
    C. eating contaminated eggs
    D. drinking contaminated water
    E. blood transfusions

12. Epidemics of giardia lamblia occurring in day care centers are USUALLY caused by

    A. inhalation of droplets
    B. person-to-person contact
    C. fecal and oral contact
    D. eating contaminated food
    E. all of the above

13. Measures of the proportion of the population exhibiting a phenomenon at a particular time is called the

    A. incidence
    B. prevalence
    C. prospective study
    D. cohort study
    E. all of the above

14. The occurrence of an event or characteristic over a period of time is called

    A. incidence
    B. prevalence
    C. specificity
    D. case control study
    E. cohort study

15. All of the following are live attenuated viral vaccines EXCEPT

    A. measles
    B. mumps
    C. rubella
    D. rabies
    E. yellow fever

16. Chlorinating air-cooling towers can prevent 16.____

    A. scarlet fever B. impetigo
    C. typhoid fever D. mycobacterium tuberculosis
    E. legionnaire's disease

17. Eliminating the disease causing agent may be done by all of the following methods EXCEPT 17.____

    A. chemotherapeutic B. cooling
    C. heating D. chlorinating
    E. disinfecting

18. Which of the following medications is used to eliminate pharyngeal carriage of neisseria meningitidis? 18.____

    A. Penicillin B. Rifampin
    C. Isoniazid D. Erythromycin
    E. Gentamicin

19. Post-exposure prophylaxis is recommended for rabies after the bite of all of the following animals EXCEPT 19.____

    A. chipmunks B. skunks C. raccoons
    D. bats E. foxes

20. To destroy the spores of clostridium botulinum, canning requires a temperature of AT LEAST _____ °C. 20.____

    A. 40 B. 60 C. 80 D. 100 E. 120

21. All of the following are killed or fractionated vaccines EXCEPT 21.____

    A. hepatitis B B. yellow fever
    C. H-influenza type B D. pneumococcus
    E. rabies

22. Of the following, the disease NOT spready by food is 22.____

    A. typhoid fever B. shigellosis
    C. typhus D. cholera
    E. legionellosis

23. In the United States, the HIGHEST attack rate of sheigella infection occurs in children between _____ of age. 23.____

    A. 1 to 6 months B. 6 months to 1 year
    C. 1 to 4 years D. 6 to 10 years
    E. 10 to 15 years

24. Risk factors for cholera include all of the following EXCEPT 24.____

    A. occupational exposure
    B. lower socioeconomic
    C. unsanitary condition
    D. high socioeconomic
    E. high population density in low income areas

25. The MOST common cause of traveler's diarrhea is
    A. escherichia coli
    B. shigella
    C. salmonella
    D. cholera
    E. campalobacter

KEY (CORRECT ANSWERS)

1. C	11. D
2. B	12. B
3. D	13. B
4. C	14. A
5. B	15. D
6. A	16. E
7. B	17. B
8. C	18. B
9. E	19. A
10. A	20. E

21. B
22. C
23. C
24. D
25. A

TEST 2

DIRECTIONS: Each question or incomplete statement is followed by several suggested answers or completions. Select the one that BEST answers the question or completes the statement. *PRINT THE LETTER OF THE CORRECT ANSWER IN THE SPACE AT THE RIGHT.*

1. The increased prevalence of entamoeba histolytica infection results from

    A. lower socioeconomic status in endemic area
    B. institutionalized (especially mentally retarded) population
    C. immigrants from endemic area
    D. promiscuous homosexual men
    E. all of the above

    1.____

2. The MOST common infection acquired in the hospital is _____ infection.

    A. surgical wound   B. lower respiratory tract
    C. urinary tract   D. bloodstream
    E. gastrointestinal

    2.____

3. The etiologic agent of Rocky Mountain spotted fever is

    A. rickettsia prowazekii   B. rickettsia rickettsii
    C. rickettsia akari   D. coxiella burnetii
    E. rochalimaena quintana

    3.____

4. The annual death rate for injuries per 100,000 in both sexes is HIGHEST in those _____ years of age.

    A. 1 to 10   B. 10 to 20   C. 30 to 40
    D. 50 to 60   E. 80 to 90

    4.____

5. The death rate per 100,000 population due to motor vehicle accident is HIGHEST among

    A. whites   B. blacks
    C. Asians   D. native Americans
    E. Spanish surnamed

    5.____

6. Among the following, the HIGHEST rate of homicide occurs in

    A. whites   B. blacks
    C. native Americans   D. Asians
    E. Spanish surnamed

    6.____

7. All of the following are true statements regarding coronary heart disease EXCEPT:

    A. About 4.6 million Americans have coronary heart disease.
    B. Men have a greater risk of MI and sudden death.
    C. Women have a greater risk of angina pectoris.
    D. 25% of coronary heart disease death occurs in individuals under the age of 65 years.
    E. White women have a greater risk of MI and sudden death.

    7.____

8. Major risk factors for coronary heart disease include all of the following EXCEPT   8._____

   A. smoking
   B. elevated blood pressure
   C. obesity
   D. high level of serum cholesterol
   E. family history of coronary heart disease

9. The MOST common cancer in American men is   9._____

   A. stomach   B. lung   C. leukemia
   D. prostate   E. skin

10. The HIGHEST incidence of prostate cancer occurs in _____ Americans.   10._____

    A. white   B. black   C. Chinese
    D. Asian   E. Spanish

11. All of the following are risk factors for cervical cancer EXCEPT   11._____

    A. smoking
    B. low socioeconomic condition
    C. first coital experience after age 20
    D. multiple sexual partners
    E. contracting a sexually transmitted disease

12. All of the following are independent adverse prognostic factors for lung cancer EXCEPT   12._____

    A. female sex
    B. short duration of symptom
    C. small cell histology
    D. metastatic disease at time of diagnosis
    E. persistently elevated CEA

13. Assuming vaccines with 80% efficacy were available in limited quantity, which vaccine among the following should be given to a military recruit?   13._____

    A. Polio   B. Pseudomonas
    C. Meningococcus   D. Influenza
    E. None of the above

14. Among the following, the vaccine which should be administered to children with sickle cell disease is   14._____

    A. influenza   B. meningococcus
    C. pseudomonas   D. pneumococcal
    E. yellow fever

15. All of the following are correct statements concerning gastric carcinoma in the United States EXCEPT: 15._____

    A. The risk for males is 2.2 times greater than for females.
    B. The incidence is increased.
    C. The risk is higher in persons with pernicious anemia than for the general population.

D. City dwellers have an increased risk of stomach cancer.
E. Workers with high levels of exposure to nickle and rubber are at increased risk.

16. During the first year of life, a condition that can be detected by screening is

   A. hypothyroidism
   B. RH incompatibility
   C. phenylketonuria
   D. congenital dislocation of the hip
   E. all of the above

17. The major reservoir of the spread of tuberculosis within a hospital is through

   A. patients
   B. custodial staff
   C. doctors
   D. nursing staff
   E. undiagnosed cases

18. All of the following statements are true regarding tuberculosis EXCEPT:

   A. Droplet nuclei are the major vehicle for the spread of tuberculosis infection.
   B. The highest incidence is among white Americans.
   C. There is a higher incidence of tuberculosis in prison than in the general population.
   D. HIV infection is a significant independent risk factor for the development of tuberculosis.
   E. A single tubercle bacillus, once having gained access to the terminal air spaces, could establish infection.

19. The human papiloma virus is associated with

   A. kaposi sarcoma
   B. hepatoma
   C. cervical neoplasia
   D. nasopharyngeal carcinoma
   E. none of the above

20. General recommendations for prevention of sexually transmitted diseases include all of the following EXCEPT

   A. contact tracing
   B. disease reporting
   C. barrier methods
   D. prophylactic antibiotic use
   E. patient education

21. Syphilis remains an important sexually transmitted disease because of all of the following EXCEPT its

   A. public health heritage
   B. effect on perinatal morbidity and mortality
   C. association with HIV transmission
   D. escalating rate among black teenagers
   E. inability to be prevented

22. Which of the following statements about homicide is NOT true? Approximately

    A. forty percent are committed by friends and acquaintances
    B. twenty percent is committed by spouse
    C. fifteen percent is committed by a member of the victim's family
    D. fifteen percent is committed by strangers
    E. fifteen percent are labeled *relationship unknown*

23. Conditions for which screening has proven cost-effective include

    A. phenylketonuria
    B. iron deficiency anemia
    C. lead poisoning
    D. tuberculosis
    E. all of the above

24. Suicide is MOST common among

    A. whites
    B. blacks
    C. hispanics
    D. Asians
    E. none of the above

25. The MOST frequenty used method of suicide is

    A. hanging
    B. poisoning by gases
    C. firearms
    D. drug overdose
    E. drowning

KEY (CORRECT ANSWERS)

1.	E	11.	C
2.	C	12.	A
3.	B	13.	C
4.	E	14.	D
5.	D	15.	B
6.	B	16.	E
7.	E	17.	E
8.	C	18.	B
9.	D	19.	C
10.	B	20.	D

21. E
22. B
23. E
24. A
25. C

EXAMINATION SECTION
TEST 1

DIRECTIONS: Each question or incomplete statement is followed by several suggested answers or completions. Select the one that BEST answers the question or completes the statement. *PRINT THE LETTER OF THE CORRECT ANSWER IN THE SPACE AT THE RIGHT.*

1. _____ accounts for the LARGEST percentage of personal health care expenditures in the United States.
    A. Physician services
    B. Hospital care
    C. Nursing homes
    D. Drug and medical supplies
    E. Dentist services

    1._____

2. MOST health care expenses in the United States are paid by
    A. government programs
    B. Medicare
    B. Medicaid
    D. private health insurance
    E. out-of-pocket payments

    2._____

3. A physician is NOT legally required to report
    A. births and deaths
    B. suspected child abuse
    C. gunshot wounds
    D. a child with croup
    E. a child with shigella dysentery

    3._____

4. Diseases more likely to occur in blacks than whites include all of the following EXCEPT
    A. thalassemia
    B. sickle cell disease
    C. sarcoidosis
    D. tuberculosis
    E. hypertension

    4._____

5. Among the United States population, what malignant tumor has the greatest incidence?
    A. Breast
    B. Prostate
    C. Lung
    D. Colon
    E. Stomach

    5._____

6. The MOST frequent cause of chronic obstructive pulmonary disease is
    A. frequent upper respiratory infection
    B. smoking
    C. family member with asthma
    D. drug abuse
    E. infantile paralysis

    6._____

7. The ultimate legal responsibility for quality of medical care provided in the hospital rests upon the
    A. hospital administrator
    B. chief of nursing staff
    C. director of the hospital
    D. principal nurse
    E. patient's physician

    7._____

45

8. Routine screening for diabetes is recommended for all patients EXCEPT those with
   A. family history of diabetes
   B. glucose abnormalities associated with pregnancy
   C. marked obesity
   D. an episode of hypoglycemia as a newborn
   E. physical abnormality, such as circulatory dysfunction and frank vascular impairment

9. Low maternal AFP level is associated with
   A. spina bifida
   B. Down syndrome
   C. meningocele
   D. hypothyroidism
   E. Niemann Pick disease

10. All of the following are skin disorders EXCEPT
    A. psoriasis
    B. eczema
    C. scleroderma
    D. gout
    E. shingles

11. All of the following are true statements regarding osteoporosis EXCEPT:
    A. The reduction of bone mass in osteoporosis causes the bone to be susceptible to fracture.
    B. Bone loss occurs with advancing age in both men and women.
    C. In developing countries, high parity has been associated with decreased bone mass and increased risk of fracture.
    D. Thin women are at higher risk than obese women.
    E. Daughters of women with osteoporosis tend to have lower bone mass than other women of their age.

12. The MOST common type of occupational disease is
    A. hearing loss
    B. dermatitis
    B. pneumoconiosis
    D. pulmonary fibrosis
    E. none of the above

13. The incidence of Down syndrome in the United States is about 1 in ____ births.
    A. 700   B. 1200   C. 1500   D. 2000   E. 10000

14. Lyme disease and Rocky Mountain spotted fever CANNOT be prevented by
    A. door and window screen use
    B. hand washing
    C. wearing protective clothing
    D. using insect repellent
    E. immediate tick removal

15. Individuals with egg allergies can be safely administered all of the following vaccines EXCEPT
    A. MMR (Measles-Mumps-Rubella)
    B. hepatitis B
    C. influenza
    D. DTaP (Diphtheria-Tetanus-Whooping Cough)
    E. none of the above

16. Lifetime prevalence of cocaine use is HIGHER among
    A. Hispanics   B. blacks   C. whites   D. Asians
    E. none of the above

17. The effectiveness of preventive measures against chronic illness is BEST determined from trends in
    A. incidence   B. mortality   C. prevalence   D. frequency of complication
    E. all of the above

18. Primary prevention of congenital heart disease includes all of the following established measures EXCEPT:
    A. Genetic counseling of potential parents and families with congenital heart disease
    B. Avoidance of exposure to viral diseases during pregnancy
    C. Avoidance of all vaccines to all children which eliminate the reservoir of infection
    D. Avoidance of radiation during pregnancy
    E. Avoidance of exposure during first trimester of pregnancy to gas fumes, air pollution, cigarettes, alcohol

19. All of the following are true statements regarding genetic factors associated with congenital heart disease EXCEPT:
    A. The offspring of a parent with a congenital heart disease has a malformation rate ranging from 1.4% to 16.1%.
    B. Identical twins are both affected 25 to 30% of the time.
    C. Single gene disorder accounts for less than 1% of all cardiac congenital anomalies.
    D. Environment does not play a role in cardiac anomalies
    E. Other finding of familial aggregation suggests polygenic factors.

20. MOST likely inadequately supplied in strict vegetarian adults is
    A. vitamin A   B. thiamin   C. vitamin B_{12} D. niacin   E. protein

21. The MOST common reservoir of acquired immune deficiency syndrome is
    A. humans   B. mosquitoes   C. cats   D. dogs   E. monkeys

22. A definitive indicator of active tuberculosis is
    A. chronic persistent cough
    B. positive PPD
    C. night sweats
    D. positive sputum test
    E. hilar adenopathy on chest x-ray

23. Which of the following is NOT a risk factor for development of colorectal carcinoma?
    A. Familial polyposis coli   B. Furcot's syndrome
    C. High fiber diet   D. Increased dietary fat
    E. Villous polyps

24. According to the American Cancer Society, starting at the age of 50, men and women at average risk for developing colorectal cancer should follow which of the following screening regimens?
    A. Colonoscopy every ten years
    B. Flexible sigmoidoscopy every two years
    C. Double-contrast barium enema every two years
    D. CT colonography (virtual colonoscopy) every year
    E. None of the above

25. The MOST common malignancy among women is of the
    A. lung   B. breast   C. ovary   D. rectum   E. vagina

KEY (CORRECT ANSWERS)

1. B
2. D
3. D
4. A
5. D
6. B
7. E
8. D
9. B
10. D

11. C
12. A
13. A
14. B
15. C
16. C
17. C
18. C
19. D
20. C

21. A
22. D
23. C
24. A
25. B

TEST 2

DIRECTIONS: Each question or incomplete statement is followed by several suggested answers or completions. Select the one that BEST answers the question or completes the statement. *PRINT THE LETTER OF THE CORRECT ANSWER IN THE SPACE AT THE RIGHT.*

1. The MOST common cause of death due to malignancy among females in the United States is from

    A. lung cancer
    B. ovarian cancer
    C. skin cancer
    D. colon and rectum cancer
    B. leukemia

1._____

2. Medicare provides health coverage to people
    A. under 20 years of age
    B. who work of all ages
    C. greater than 65 years of age and end-stage renal dialysis patients
    D. under five years of age who require long-term hospitalization
    E. who need out-patient care only

2._____

3. Insurance approaches to contain cost include managed care plans. A popular managed care approach has been
    A. Medicare
    B. Medicaid
    C. HMO's
    D. institutional reimbursement
    E. none of the above

3._____

4. The occupational exposure that may lead to chronic interstitial pulmonary disease is
    A. silicosis
    B. pneumoconiosis
    C. asbestosis
    D. farmer's lung
    E. all of the above

4._____

5. The principal mode of transmission of hepatitis A virus is
    A. blood transfusion
    B. droplet nuclei
    C. fecal and oral route
    D. mosquitoes
    E. deer flies

5._____

6. The leading cause of death among diabetics after 20 years of diabetes is by
    A. infection
    B. cerebrovascular accident
    C. renal and cardiovascular disease
    D. diabetic ketoacidosis
    E. malignancy

6._____

7. A breast-fed infant may require a supplementation of vitamin
    A. E   B. B_{12} C. K   D. D   E. A

7._____

8. The MOST common organism associated with chronic active gastritis is
    A. salmonella
    B. shigella
    C. campylobacter pylori
    D. staphylococcus
    E. rota virus

8._____

49

9. The large proportion of tuberculosis in older persons is due to   9._____
   A. recent exposure to tuberculosis
   B. reactivation of latent infection
   C. malnutrition
   D. immunosuppression
   E. substance abuse

10. The leading vector-borne disease in the United States is   10._____
    A. lyme disease
    B. Rocky Mountain spotted fever
    C. ehrlichiosis
    D. Q fever
    E. yellow fever

11. The malarial species causing the MOST fatal illness is   11._____
    A. P. vivax   B. P. falciparum
    C. P. malariae   D. P. cuale
    E. none of the above

Questions 12-16.

DIRECTIONS: Match the disease in Questions 12 through 16 with the associated animal in Column I.

12. Brucellosis	COLUMN I	12._____
13. Psittacosis	A. Bird	13._____
	B. Swine	
14. Rabies	C. Rabbit	14._____
	D. Skunk	
15. Tularemia	E. Cats	15._____
16. Toxoplasmosis		16._____

Questions 17-22.

DIRECTIONS: Match the trade in Questions 17 through 22 with the related occupational cancer in Column I.

17. Pipefitters

18. Rubber industry workers

19. Radiologist

20. Woodworkers

21. Textile workers

22. Chemists

COLUMN I

A. Carcinoma of the bladder
B. Mesothelioma
C. Hodgkin's disease
D. Leukemia
E. Brain cancer
F. Carcinoma of nasal cavity

17.____
18.____
19.____
20.____
21.____
22.____

Questions 23-25.

DIRECTIONS: Match the biostatistical description in Questions 23 through 25 with the related term in Column I.

23. The presence of an event or characteristic at a single point in time

24. Require a long period of observation

25. The occurrence of an event or characteristic over a period of time

COLUMN I

A. Incidence
B. Prevalence
C. Cohort study

23.____
24.____
25.____

KEY (CORRECT ANSWERS)

1. A
2. C
3. C
4. E
5. C
6. C
7. D
8. C
9. B
10. A

11. B
12. B
13. A
14. D
15. C
16. E
17. B
18. A
19. D
20. C

21. F
22. E
23. B
24. C
25. A

EXAMINATION SECTION
TEST 1

DIRECTIONS: Each question or incomplete statement is followed by several suggested answers or completions. Select the one that BEST answers the question or completes the statement. *PRINT THE LETTER OF THE CORRECT ANSWER IN THE SPACE AT THE RIGHT.*

1. A PPD reaction of greater than or equal to 5 mm induration is considered positive in all of the following individuals EXCEPT

    A. persons with HIV infection
    B. IV drug abusers who are HIV antibody negative
    C. close recent contacts of an infectious tuberculosis case
    D. persons with a chest radiograph consistent with old, healed tuberculosis
    E. persons with HIV infection or with risk factors for HIV infection who have an unknown IV antibody status

2. All of the following are true about tuberculosis EXCEPT:

    A. The causative agent is M. tuberculosis var. hominis
    B. It is more likely to occur in older individuals (more than 45 years of age)
    C. It is more common in non-whites than in whites
    D. It is more common in men than in women
    E. About 90% of cases in the United States represent new infections

3. The groups that should benefit from preventive therapy for tuberculosis include all of the following EXCEPT

    A. individuals whose skin test has converted from negative to positive in the previous 2 years
    B. individuals with positive mantoux test and with HIV infection
    C. tuberculin-negative IV drug abusers
    D. tuberculin-positive individuals under 35 years of age
    E. individuals with immunosuppressive therapy who are tuberculin positive

4. INH prophylaxis should not be used in any of the following EXCEPT in

    A. the presence of clinical disease
    B. a pregnant woman who has recently converted to tuberculin positive
    C. patients with unstable hepatic function
    D. individuals who were previously adequately treated
    E. individuals with a previous adverse reaction to INH

5. What is the MOST common cause of bacterial meningitis in children under age 5?

    A. Streptococcus pneumoniae
    B. H. influenza
    C. N. meningitidis
    D. E. coli
    E. Staphylococcus aureus

6. All of the following are true about H. influenza infection EXCEPT:

    A. Peak incidence is from age 3 months to 2 years
    B. The mortality rate is about 5%
    C. Secondary spread to day care contacts under 4 years of age is rare
    D. About two-thirds of the cases occur in children under 15 months of age
    E. None of the above

7. All of the following statements are true about hemophilus influenza type B infection EXCEPT:

    A. Rifampin is the drug of choice for chemoprophylaxis
    B. Rifampin may be given to pregnant women
    C. The disease is more common in native and black Americans
    D. Humans are the reservoir of infections
    E. None of the above

8. All of the following statements are true about meningococcal meningitis EXCEPT:

    A. It is the second most common cause of bacterial meningitis in the United States
    B. The peak incidence is around age 6-12 months
    C. Most cases occur in late winter and early spring
    D. The portal of entry is not the nasopharynx
    E. It is more likely to occur in newly aggregated young adults who are living in institutions and barracks

9. Antimicrobial chemoprophylaxis is the chief preventive measure in sporadic cases of meningococcal meningitis and should be offered to

    A. household contacts
    B. day care center contacts
    C. medical personnel who resuscitated, intubated or suctioned the patient before antibiotics were instituted
    D. all patients who were treated for meningococcal disease before discharge from the hospital
    E. all of the above

10. What is the MOST common cause of bacterial meningitis in children under 5 years of age?

    A. Streptococcus pneumoniae
    B. Nisseriae meningitidis
    C. Listeria monocytogenes
    D. Group B streptococcus
    E. Hemophilus influenza type B

11. All of the following are true about coronary heart disease EXCEPT:

    A. It is the leading cause of death in the United States
    B. About 4.6 million Americans have coronary heart disease
    C. It is most common in white men
    D. Women have a greater risk of myocardial infarction and sudden death
    E. Women have a greater risk of angina pectoris

12. According to the National Cholesterol Education Panel, which of the following is NOT a major risk factor for coronary artery disease?

    A. Women 55 years and older
    B. Hypertension
    C. Individuals with diabetes mellitus
    D. High density lipoprotein (HDL) less than 35 mg/dl
    E. Obesity

13. The number one cause of cancer death in the United States is _____ cancer.

    A. lung   B. breast   C. colorectal
    D. cervical   E. prostatic

14. The MOST common cancer in American men is _____ cancer.

    A. lung   B. breast   C. prostate
    D. colon   E. esophageal

15. All of the following are risk factors for women to develop breast cancer EXCEPT

    A. exposure to ionizing radiation
    B. becoming pregnant for the first time after age 30
    C. mother and sisters having breast cancer
    D. high socioeconomic status
    E. late menarchae

16. Cervical cancer is one of the leading causes of death among women. Of the following, which is NOT a risk factor for developing cervical cancer?

    A. Multiple sexual partners
    B. First coitus before age 20
    C. Low socioeconomic status
    D. Oral contraceptive use
    E. Partners of uncircumcised men

17. Population subgroups at INCREASED risk of developing anemia include

    A. women   B. elderly men
    C. children   D. blacks
    E. all of the above

18. Uncontrolled hypertensive disease increases the risk of developing all of the following disorders EXCEPT

    A. coronary heart disease   B. diabetes mellitus
    C. renal disease   D. cerebrovascular disease
    E. none of the above

19. All of the following statements are true regarding chronic obstructive pulmonary disease (COPD) EXCEPT:

    A. Men are at higher risk than women
    B. An estimated 16 million Americans have chronic bronchitis, asthma or emphysema
    C. The risk is related to the duration of smoking only

D. The risk is related to the number of cigarettes smoked daily and to the duration of smoking
E. Offspring of affected individuals are at higher risk

20. Which of the following statements is TRUE regarding diabetes in the United States?

    A. It accounts for 5% of all deaths.
    B. Its prevalence is estimated at 15%.
    C. 80% of all diabetics have the non-insulin dependent type.
    D. It is the leading cause of blindness.
    E. Men are at greater risk than women.

21. People with increased risk for suicide include all of the following EXCEPT

    A. drug users
    B. married individuals
    C. teenagers
    D. chronically depressed
    E. homosexuals

22. Conditions associated with an increased risk for suicide include all of the following EXCEPT

    A. unemployed
    B. seriously physically ill or handicapped
    C. chronically mentally ill
    D. substance abusers
    E. none of the above

23. The leading cause of death among black men aged 15-24 years is

    A. automobile accidents
    B. homicide
    C. cancer
    D. drug abuse
    E. AIDS

24. All of the following are true regarding pernicious anemia EXCEPT:

    A. It primarily affects individuals over the age of 30
    B. The incidence increases with age
    C. It is more common in Asians and blacks
    D. It is caused by a vitamin B_{12} deficiency
    E. None of the above

25. Which of the following groups of individuals have a high risk of injuries?

    A. Factory workers
    B. Alcoholics
    C. Individuals with osteoporosis
    D. Homeless
    E. All of the above

KEY (CORRECT ANSWERS)

1.	B	11.	D
2.	E	12.	D
3.	C	13.	A
4.	B	14.	C
5.	B	15.	E
6.	C	16.	C
7.	B	17.	E
8.	D	18.	B
9.	E	19.	C
10.	E	20.	D

21. B
22. E
23. B
24. C
25. E

TEST 2

DIRECTIONS: Each question or incomplete statement is followed by several suggested answers or completions. Select the one that BEST answers the question or completes the statement. *PRINT THE LETTER OF THE CORRECT ANSWER IN THE SPACE AT THE RIGHT.*

1. Which of the following factors does NOT increase a woman's risk of an ectopic pregnancy?   1.____

   A. Progestin exposure
   B. Pelvic inflammatory disease
   C. Smoking
   D. Use of alcohol
   E. Infertility

2. Breastfeeding usually enhances all of the following EXCEPT   2.____

   A. bonding between mother and infant
   B. infant nutrition
   C. immune defenses
   D. antibody response against HIV virus
   E. return of uterus to prepregnant size

3. Which of the following is NOT a leading cause of maternal mortality in the United States?   3.____

   A. Hypertensive disease of pregnancy
   B. Cardiovascular accidents
   C. Miscarriage
   D. Anesthesia complications
   E. All of the above

4. A well-woman prenatal visit should include all of the following EXCEPT a(n)   4.____

   A. weight check
   B. blood pressure check
   C. electronic fetal monitoring
   D. pap smear
   E. urine analysis

5. All of the following substances or conditions are harmful to the fetus during gestation EXCEPT   5.____

   A. tetracycline   B. alcohol   C. herpes
   D. rubella   E. thalidomide

6. The use of an intrauterine device (IUD) has been associated with increased risk of   6.____

   A. ectopic pregnancy
   B. pelvic inflammatory disease
   C. infertility
   D. infections
   E. all of the above

58

7. The number of deaths among infants less than 28 days old per 1,000 live births is called the _____ mortality rate.   7._____

   A. neonatal B. post-neonatal
   C. fetal D. perinatal
   E. none of the above

8. All of the following are causes of postneonatal mortality EXCEPT   8._____

   A. lower respiratory tract infections
   B. intrauterine growth retardation
   C. congenital anomalies
   D. sudden infant death syndrome
   E. injuries, e.g., motor vehicle accidents

9. All of the following are important factors in the identification of high risk parents and in the management and prevention of infant health problems EXCEPT   9._____

   A. intrauterine infections
   B. pre-existing maternal illnesses
   C. paternal age
   D. maternal history of reproductive problems
   E. family history of hereditary disease

10. Screening for which of the following conditions has been proven to be cost effective?   10._____

    A. Phenylketonuria B. Congenital hypothyroidism
    C. Lead poisoning D. Tuberculosis
    E. All of the above

11. Children _____ are more likely to receive inadequate well-child care.   11._____

    A. with chronic health problems
    B. on medicaid
    C. of mothers who started receiving prenatal care late in the second or third trimester
    D. of parents whose jobs do not provide health insurance
    E. all of the above

12. Injuries are classified by the intent or purposefulness of occurrence. All of the following are classified as intentional injuries EXCEPT   12._____

    A. child abuse B. motor vehicle mishaps
    C. sexual assault D. domestic violence
    E. abuse of the elderly

13. Schizophrenia is a disorder, or group of disorders, with a variety of symptoms that include   13._____

    A. delusions B. hallucinations
    C. agitation D. apathy
    E. all of the above

14. All of the following are true about the incidence and prevalence of bipolar disorder EXCEPT: 14._____

A. Approximately 4-5% of the population is at risk
B. More women are admitted to the hospital with the diagnosis of bipolar disorder than men
C. The manic form occurs primarily in younger individuals
D. Bipolar patients are more likely to be unmarried
E. The depressive form occurs primarily in older individuals

15. In schizophrenia, there is an increased risk for all of the following EXCEPT

    A. malabsorption syndrome
    B. arteriosclerotic heart disease
    C. hypothyroidism
    D. cancer
    E. none of the above

16. A 6-month-old Jewish infant has a history of seizures, progressive blindness, deafness, and paralysis with an exaggerated startle response to sound.
    The MOST likely diagnosis is

    A. phenylketonuria   B. Gaucher's disease
    C. Tay Sachs disease   D. homocystinuria
    E. maple syrup disease

17. The MOST common inborn error of amino acid metabolism results in

    A. phenylketonuria   B. maple syrup disease
    C. homocystinuria   D. albinism
    E. Gaucher's disease

18. The MOST common lysosomal storage disease is

    A. Niemann-Pick disease   B. Gaucher's disease
    C. Tay Sachs disease   D. homocystinuria
    E. none of the above

19. All of the following are true about spina bifida EXCEPT:

    A. The most common type is spina bifida occulta
    B. The least severe form is myelocoele
    C. Encephalocoele is the rarest type
    D. The most common site affected is lower back
    E. The familial risk of recurrence is approximately 5%

Questions 20-25.

DIRECTIONS: For each metal listed in Questions 20 through 25, select the condition in the column below that is MOST likely to result from chronic exposure to it.

20. Lead   A. Osteomalacia-like disease
21. Arsenic   B. Granulomas of skin and lungs
22. Cadmium   C. Abnormal sperms
23. Mercury   D. Nasal septal ulceration
24. Beryllium   E. Visual field abnormalities
25. Zinc   F. Metal fume fever

KEY (CORRECT ANSWERS)

1. D
2. D
3. C
4. C
5. C

6. E
7. A
8. B
9. C
10. E

11. E
12. B
13. E
14. D
15. D

16. C
17. A
18. C
19. B
20. C

21. D
22. A
23. E
24. B
25. F

EXAMINATION SECTION
TEST 1

DIRECTIONS: Each question or incomplete statement is followed by several suggested answers or completions. Select the one that BEST answers the question or completes the statement. *PRINT THE LETTER OF THE CORRECT ANSWER IN THE SPACE AT THE RIGHT.*

1. The abbreviation *EEG* refers to a(n)

    A. examination of the eyes and ears
    B. inflammatory disease of the urinogenital tract
    C. disease of the esophageal structure
    D. examination of the brain

2. The complete destruction of all forms of living microorganisms is called

    A. decontamination B. sterilization
    C. fumigation   D. germination

3. A rectal thermometer differs from other fever thermometers in that it has a

    A. longer stem   B. thinner stem
    C. stubby bulb at one end D. slender bulb at one end

4. The one of the following pieces of equipment which is USUALLY used together with a sphygmometer is a

    A. stethoscope   B. watch
    C. fever thermometer   D. hypodermic syringe

5. A curette is a

    A. healing drug   B. curved scalpel
    C. long hypodermic needle D. scraping instrument

6. The otoscope is used to examine the patient's

    A. eyes   B. ears   C. mouth   D. lungs

7. A catheter is used

    A. to close wounds
    B. for withdrawing fluid from a body cavity
    C. to remove cataracts
    D. as a cathartic

8. Of the following pieces of equipment, the one that is required for making a scratch test is a

    A. needle   B. scalpel   C. capillary tube   D. tourniquet

9. A hemostat is an instrument which is used to

    A. hold a sterile needle
    B. clamp off a blood vessel
    C. regulate the temperature of a sterilizer
    D. measure oxygen intake

63

10. Of the following medical supplies, the one that MUST be stored in a tightly sealed bottle is

    A. sodium fluoride
    B. alum
    C. oil of cloves
    D. aromatic spirits of ammonia

11. A person who has been exposed to an infectious disease is called

    A. a contact
    B. an incubator
    C. diseased
    D. infected

12. A myocardial infarct would occur in the

    A. heart   B. kidneys   C. lungs   D. spleen

13. The abbreviations *WBC* and *RBC* refer to the results of tests of the

    A. basal metabolism
    B. blood
    C. blood pressure
    D. bony structure

14. When a person's blood pressure is noted as 120/80, it means that his

    A. pulse blood pressure is 120
    B. pulse blood pressure is 80
    C. systolic blood pressure is 120
    D. systolic blood pressure is 80

15. The anatomical structure that contains the tonsils and adenoids is the

    A. pharynx   B. larynx   C. trachea   D. sinuses

16. An abscess can BEST be described as a

    A. loss of sensation
    B. painful tooth
    C. ruptured membrane
    D. localized formation of pus

17. Nephritis is a disease affecting the

    A. gall bladder
    B. larynx
    C. kidney
    D. large intestine

18. Hemoglobin is contained in the

    A. white blood cells
    B. lymph fluids
    C. platelets
    D. red blood cells

19. Bile is a body fluid that is MOST directly concerned with

    A. digestion
    B. excretion
    C. reproduction
    D. metabolism

20. Of the following bones, the one which is located BELOW the waist is the

    A. sternum   B. clavicle   C. tibia   D. humerus

21. The one of the following which is NOT part of the digestive canal is the

    A. esophagus   B. larynx   C. duodenum   D. colon

22. The thyroid and the pituitary are part of the _____ system.

    A. digestive   B. endocrine
    C. respiratory   D. excretory

23. The one of the following which would be included in a *GU* examination is the

    A. rectum   B. trachea   C. kidneys   D. pancreas

24. Of the following, the one which would be included in the x-ray examination known as a *GI series* is the

    A. colon   B. skull   C. lungs   D. uterus

25. A person who, while not ill himself, may transmit a disease to another person is known as a(n)

    A. breeder   B. incubator
    C. carrier   D. inhibitor

KEY (CORRECT ANSWERS)

1.	D	11.	A
2.	C	12.	A
3.	C	13.	B
4.	A	14.	C
5.	D	15.	A
6.	B	16.	D
7.	B	17.	C
8.	A	18.	D
9.	B	19.	A
10.	D	20.	C

21. B
22. B
23. C
24. A
25. C

TEST 2

DIRECTIONS: Each question or incomplete statement is followed by several suggested answers or completions. Select the one that BEST answers the question or completes the statement. *PRINT THE LETTER OF THE CORRECT ANSWER IN THE SPACE AT THE RIGHT.*

1. Thorough washing of the hands for two minutes with soap and warm water will leave the hands 1.____

    A. sterile
    B. aseptic
    C. decontaminated
    D. partially disinfected

2. The one of the following which is BEST for preparing the skin for an injection is 2.____

    A. green soap and water
    B. alcohol
    C. phenol
    D. formalin

3. A fever thermometer should be cleansed after use by washing it with 3.____

    A. soap and cool water
    B. warm water only
    C. soap and hot water
    D. running cold tap water

4. The FIRST step in cleaning an instrument which has fresh blood on it is to 4.____

    A. wash it in hot soapy water
    B. wash it under cool running water
    C. soak it in a boric acid bath
    D. soak it in 70% alcohol

5. If a contaminated nasal speculum cannot be sterilized immediately after use, then the BEST procedure to follow until sterilization is possible is to place it 5.____

    A. under a piece of dry *gauze*
    B. in warm water
    C. in alcohol
    D. in a green soap solution

6. A hypodermic needle should ALWAYS be checked to see whether it has a good sharp point 6.____

    A. when it is being washed
    B. when it is removed from the sterilizer
    C. just before it is sterilized
    D. immediately before an injection

7. Of the following, the LOWEST temperature at which cotton goods will be sterilized if placed in an autoclave for 30 minutes is 7.____

    A. 130° F   B. 170° F   C. 200° F   D. 250° F

8. Of the following procedures, the one which is BEST for sterilizing an ear speculum which is contaminated with wax is to

   A. scrub it with cold soapy water, rinse in ether, and place in boiling water for 20 minutes
   B. soak it in warm water, scrub in cold soapy water, rinse with water, and autoclave at 275° F for 10 minutes
   C. wash it in alcohol, scrub in hot soapy water, rinse with water, and place in boiling water for 20 minutes
   D. wash it in 1% Lysol solution, rinse, and autoclave at 275° F for 15 minutes

9. Assume that clean water accidentally spilled on the outside of a package of cloth-wrapped hypodermic syringes which has been sterilized.
   Of the following, the BEST action to take is to

   A. leave the package to dry in a sunny, clean place
   B. sterilize the package again
   C. remove the wet cloth and wrap the package in a dry sterile cloth
   D. wipe off the package with a clean dry towel and later ask the nurse-in-charge what to do

10. Hypodermic needles should be sterilized by placing them in

    A. boiling water for 5 minutes
    B. an autoclave at 15 lbs. pressure for 15 minutes
    C. oil heated to 220° F for 10 minutes
    D. a 1:40 Lysol solution for 10 minutes

11. A cutting instrument should be sterilized by placing it in

    A. a chemical germicide
    B. an autoclave at 15 lbs. pressure for 20 minutes
    C. boiling water for 20 minutes
    D. a hot air oven at 320° F for 1 hour

12. A fever thermometer used by a patient who has tuberculosis should be washed and then placed in

    A. boiling water for 10 minutes
    B. a hot air oven for 20 minutes
    C. a 1:1000 solution of bichloride of mercury for one minute
    D. an autoclave at 15 lbs. pressure for 15 minutes

13. The MOST reliable method of sterilizing a glass syringe is to place it in

    A. Zephiran chloride 1:1000 solution for 40 minutes
    B. oil heated to 250° F for 12 minutes
    C. boiling water for 20 minutes
    D. an autoclave at 15 lbs. pressure for 20 minutes

14. The insides of sterilizers should be cleaned daily with a mild abrasive PRIMARILY to   14._____

    A. remove scale
    B. prevent the growth of bacteria
    C. remove blood and other organic matter
    D. prevent acids from damaging the sterilizer

15. Of the following, the BEST reason for giving a patient a jar in which to bring a urine specimen on his next visit to the clinic is that the   15._____

    A. patient may not have a jar at home
    B. patient may bring the specimen in a jar which is too large
    C. patient may bring the specimen in a jar which has not been cleaned properly
    D. jar may be misplaced if it is not a jar in which urine specimens are usually collected

16. Of the following, the MOST important reason why you should remain with a 4-year-old child when his temperature is being taken by mouth is that otherwise the child might   16._____

    A. fall off the chair and fracture an arm or leg
    B. break the thermometer while it is in his mouth
    C. remove the thermometer from his mouth and misplace it
    D. leave the examining room and return to his mother

17. The BEST way to take the temperature of an infant is by   17._____

    A. feeling his forehead
    B. using an oral thermometer
    C. placing a thermometer under his armpit
    D. using a rectal thermometer

18. When the temperature of an adult is taken rectally, it is LEAST accurate to say that the   18._____

    A. temperature reading will be higher than if it were taken orally
    B. thermometer should be lubricated before use
    C. thermometer should be in place for at least ten minutes
    D. temperature reading is likely to be more accurate than if it were taken orally

19. When the temperature of an adult is taken orally, it is LEAST accurate to say that the   19._____

    A. thermometer should be washed with alcohol before it is used
    B. thermometer should be taken down below 96° F before it is used
    C. patient's temperature may be taken immediately after he has smoked a cigarette
    D. patient should be inactive just before his temperature is taken

20. The nurse described the test to the patient before bringing him to the examining room for a basal metabolism test. Her action may BEST be described as   20._____

    A. *correct;* the patient will be more cooperative if he knows what to expect
    B. *wrong;* the nurse does not know how the test will affect the patient
    C. *correct;* the nurse can judge whether the patient is too upset by this information to take the test
    D. *wrong;* explaining the test beforehand will only make the patient nervous

21. When a patient's sputum test is *positive,* it means that the 21.____

    A. patient's sputum is plentiful
    B. doctor has made an accurate diagnosis
    C. patient has recovered and is now in good health
    D. laboratory reports that the patient's sputum contains certain disease germs

22. A biopsy can BEST be described as a(n) 22.____

    A. pre-cancerous condition   B. examination of tissues
    C. living organism   D. germicidal solution

23. The *scratch* or *patch* test is USUALLY given when testing for 23.____

    A. allergies   B. rheumatic fever
    C. blood poisoning   D. diabetes

24. Gamma globulin is frequently given to children after exposure to and before the appearance of symptoms of 24.____

    A. measles   B. smallpox
    C. tetanus   D. chicken pox

25. Of the following, the one which is NOT a respiratory disease is 25.____

    A. bronchitis   B. pneumonia
    C. nephritis   D. croup

KEY (CORRECT ANSWERS)

1.	D	11.	A
2.	B	12.	C
3.	A	13.	D
4.	B	14.	A
5.	D	15.	C
6.	C	16.	B
7.	D	17.	D
8.	C	18.	C
9.	B	19.	C
10.	B	20.	A

21. D
22. B
23. A
24. A
25. C

TEST 3

DIRECTIONS: Each question or incomplete statement is followed by several suggested answers or completions. Select the one that BEST answers the question or completes the statement. *PRINT THE LETTER OF THE CORRECT ANSWER IN THE SPACE AT THE RIGHT.*

1. A physician who specializes in the treatment of conditions affecting the skin is known as a(n)   1.____
    A. urologist
    B. dermatologist
    C. toxicologist
    D. ophthalmologist

2. The branch of medicine which deals with diseases peculiar to women is   2.____
    A. pathology
    B. orthopedics
    C. neurology
    D. gynecology

3. The branch of medicine which deals with diseases of old age is called   3.____
    A. pediatrics
    B. geriatrics
    C. serology
    D. histology

4. *Petit mal* is a form of   4.____
    A. epilepsy   B. syphilis   C. diabetes   D. malaria

5. Glaucoma is a disease of the   5.____
    A. thyroid gland
    B. liver
    C. bladder
    D. eye

6. A patient who has edema has   6.____
    A. not enough red blood cells
    B. too much water in the body tissues
    C. blood in the urine
    D. a swollen gland

7. The thoracic area of the body is located in the   7.____
    A. abdomen
    B. lower back
    C. chest
    D. neck

8. An electrocardiograph is MOST usually used in the examination of the   8.____
    A. brain
    B. heart
    C. kidney
    D. gall bladder

9. The word *coagulate* means MOST NEARLY to   9.____
    A. bleed excessively
    B. break up
    C. work together
    D. form a clot

10. A stethoscope is used to examine the patient's   10.____
    A. heart
    B. patellar reflex
    C. blood cells
    D. spinal fluid

11. A pelvimeter is MOST usually used in the examination of a patient in the _____ clinic. 11._____

    A. chest   B. cancer   C. prenatal   D. eye

12. Tuberculin may BEST be described as a 12._____

    A. virus infection of the lungs
    B. preparation used in the diagnosis of tuberculosis
    C. sanitarium for tuberculous patients
    D. form of cancer of the lung

13. An autoclave is a(n) 13._____

    A. automatic dispenser of instruments needed for clinic examinations
    B. sterile place for storing clinic supplies until they are needed
    C. apparatus for sterilizing equipment under steam pressure
    D. portable self-operating general anesthesia unit

14. Radiation therapy is 14._____

    A. the recording of electrical impulses of the body on a graph
    B. a study of the effects of radiation fall-out on the human body
    C. a form of treatment used for certain diseases
    D. the filming of internal parts of the body through the use of x-rays

15. Diathermy is the treatment of patients by 15._____

    A. scientific use of baths and mineral waters
    B. insertion of radium into diseased tissues
    C. intravenous feedings of vitamins and minerals
    D. electrical generation of heat in the body tissues

16. The measurement of blood pressure involves two readings, which are known as 16._____

    A. metabolic and diastolic
    B. systolic and diastolic
    C. metabolic and hyperbolic
    D. hyperbolic and systolic

17. The Snellen chart is used in examinations of the 17._____

    A. eyes   B. blood   C. urine   D. bile

18. An enema is MOST generally used to 18._____

    A. induce vomiting
    B. irrigate the stomach
    C. clear the bowels
    D. drain the urinary bladder

19. A bronchoscope is USUALLY used in examinations of the 19._____

    A. kidneys   B. heart   C. stomach   D. lungs

20. The Wassermann test is used to find out whether a patient has

   A. diphtheria B. leukemia
   C. scarlet fever D. syphilis

21. If a boiling water sterilizer is used, the minimum time necessary to sterilize instruments is MOST NEARLY _____ hour(s).

   A. 1/2   B. 1   C. 1 1/2   D. 2

22. To sterilize towels and dry gauze dressings in the health clinic, it is MOST advisable to

   A. dip them in a sterilizing solution
   B. wash them with a strong detergent
   C. boil them in the sterilizer
   D. steam them under pressure

23. Sterilization by use of chemicals rather than by boiling water is indicated when the instrument

   A. is made of soft rubber
   B. has a sharp cutting edge
   C. has pus or blood on it
   D. was used more than 24 hours before sterilization

24. When dusting the furniture in the clinic, it is advisable to use a silicone-treated dustcloth CHIEFLY because the treated cloth will

   A. collect the dust more efficiently
   B. disinfect as well as dust the furniture
   C. not remove the wax from the furniture
   D. make it unnecessary to polish the furniture in the future

25. Assume that the clinic in which you work has issued instructions that all supplies containing poison are to have blue labels with the word *poison* clearly marked on the label, and that these supplies are to be kept in a storage cabinet separate from other supplies. You notice that a bottle with no label is on a shelf in the *poison* storage cabinet.
    Of the following, the BEST action for you to take is to

   A. place the unlabeled bottle in the back of the regular storage cabinet
   B. put a blue label on the bottle and write *poison* on the label
   C. ask another public health employee to help you decide if the bottle contains poison
   D. pour the contents of the bottle into the slop sink and destroy the bottle

KEY (CORRECT ANSWERS)

1. B
2. D
3. B
4. A
5. D

6. B
7. C
8. B
9. D
10. A

11. C
12. B
13. C
14. C
15. D

16. B
17. A
18. C
19. D
20. D

21. A
22. D
23. B
24. A
25. D

TEST 4

DIRECTIONS: Each question or incomplete statement is followed by several suggested answers or completions. Select the one that BEST answers the question or completes the statement. *PRINT THE LETTER OF THE CORRECT ANSWER IN THE SPACE AT THE RIGHT.*

1. When storing medical supplies, it is important to remember that liquids should be labeled   1.____

    A. only if the liquids are poisonous and there is the slightest chance that they will not be recognized
    B. whenever there is the slightest chance that they will not be recognized
    C. at all times and discarded if labels have become detached
    D. only in those cases where the liquids will be given to patients

2. When dusting metal counter tops in the clinic, it is BEST to use a clean cloth which is   2.____

    A. medicated   B. wet   C. dry   D. damp

3. Of the following statements concerning a hypodermic syringe, the one that is MOST correct is that a plunger   3.____

    A. used for taking blood specimens can be used with any syringe barrel
    B. can be used for any syringe barrel as long as it goes in easily
    C. can be used only with the syringe barrel that was made for it
    D. must be used with the syringe barrel that was made for it only if it is to be used for injections

4. The one of the following which should NOT be done when using a thermometer is to   4.____

    A. shake down the thermometer to 95° F before taking the patient's temperature
    B. ask the patient to keep his lips closed when taking the temperature orally
    C. wash the thermometer in hot soapy water after use
    D. keep the thermometer in a container of alcohol when not in use

5. The temperature of an adult when taken by rectum is USUALLY   5.____

    A. *higher* than if taken either by mouth or under the armpit
    B. *higher* than if taken by mouth and lower than if taken under the armpit
    C. *lower* than if taken either by mouth or under the armpit
    D. *lower* than if taken by mouth and higher than if taken under the armpit

6. Of the following tests, the one which is associated with tuberculosis is the _____ test.   6.____

    A. Schick   B. Mantoux   C. Dick   D. Kahn

7. A needle that has been used to draw blood should be rinsed immediately after use in   7.____

    A. a disinfectant solution   B. hot water
    C. cold water   D. hot, soapy water

8. Of the following, the statement that is MOST correct is that a hypodermic needle should be checked for burrs, hooks, and sharpness   8._____

   A. once a week
   B. before it is sterilized
   C. after it has been sterilized
   D. after it has been used three or four times

9. The MOST accurate of the following statements is that when a syringe and needle are being sterilized by boiling, the   9._____

   A. plunger must be completely out of the barrel
   B. needle should be left attached to the barrel as when in use
   C. plunger may be completely inside the barrel
   D. needle should be boiled at least twice as long as the syringe

10. Of the following, the MOST important reason for washing an instrument in hot, soapy water is to   10._____

    A. sterilize the instrument
    B. destroy germs by heat
    C. destroy germs by coagulation
    D. remove foreign matter and bacteria

11. Assume that a hypodermic needle which is to be used for injection is accidentally brushed at the tip by your hand. Of the following, the action which should be taken before this needle is used is that it be   11._____

    A. washed under the hot water tap
    B. wiped with a sterile piece of gauze
    C. washed in hot, soapy water, then rinsed in sterile water
    D. boiled for ten minutes

12. The CORRECT way to sterilize a scalpel is to   12._____

    A. place it in a chemical germicide
    B. boil it for 10 minutes
    C. put it in the autoclave
    D. pass it through a bright flame

13. Assume that a tray of instruments has been accidentally left uncovered for five minutes after it had been sterilized.
    Of the following, the action you should take to ensure that the instruments are sterile for use is to   13._____

    A. dip them in boiling water
    B. boil them for 10 minutes
    C. replace the cover on the tray
    D. wipe each instrument with sterile gauze

14. An intramuscular injection is MOST likely to be used in the administration of   14._____

    A. smallpox vaccine   B. streptomycin
    C. glucose   D. blood

15. The one of the following which is NOT a normal element of blood is   15.____

    A. hemoglobin   B. a leucocyte
    C. marrow   D. a platelet

16. Of the following statements regarding the Salk vaccine, the MOST accurate one is that it   16.____

    A. immunizes children and adults against paralytic poliomyelit is
    B. is a test to determine the presence of poliomyelitis virus in the blood
    C. is a test to determine whether a child is immune to poliomyelitis
    D. is used in the treatment of patients suffering from paralytic poliomyelitis

17. The GREATEST success in the treatment of cancer has been in cancer of the   17.____

    A. blood   B. stomach   C. liver   D. skin

18. An autopsy is a(n)   18.____

    A. type of blood test
    B. examination of tissue removed from a living organism
    C. examination of a human body after death
    D. test to determine the acidity of body fluids

19. The word *vascular* is MOST closely associated with   19.____

    A. the circulatory system   B. respiration
    C. digestion   D. the nervous system

20. The word *diagnosis* means MOST NEARLY   20.____

    A. preparation of a diagram
    B. determination of an illness
    C. medical examination of a patient
    D. written prescription

21. A tendon connects   21.____

    A. bone to bone   B. muscle to bone
    C. muscle to muscle   D. muscle to ligament

22. Blood takes on oxygen as it passes through the   22.____

    A. liver   B. heart   C. spleen   D. lungs

23. The fatty substance in the blood which is deposited in the artery walls and which is believed to cause hardening of the arteries is called   23.____

    A. amino acid   B. phenol
    C. cholesterol   D. pectin

24. The digestive canal includes the   24.____

    A. stomach, small intestine, large intestine, and rectum
    B. stomach, larynx, large intestine, and rectum
    C. trachea, small intestine, large intestine, and rectum
    D. stomach, small intestine, large intestine, and abdominal cavity

25. When giving artificial respiration, it should be kept in mind that air is drawn into the lungs   25._____
    by the
    A. expansion of the chest cavity
    B. contraction of the chest cavity
    C. expansion of the lungs
    D. contraction of the lungs

KEY (CORRECT ANSWERS)

1.	C	11.	D
2.	D	12.	A
3.	C	13.	B
4.	C	14.	B
5.	A	15.	C
6.	B	16.	A
7.	C	17.	D
8.	B	18.	C
9.	A	19.	A
10.	D	20.	B

21. B
22. D
23. C
24. A
25. A

EXAMINATION SECTION
TEST 1

DIRECTIONS: Each question or incomplete statement is followed by several suggested answers or completions. Select the one that BEST answers the question or completes the statement. *PRINT THE LETTER OF THE CORRECT ANSWER IN THE SPACE AT THE RIGHT.*

1. Those who are legally entitled to view a client's medical records without written consent include
    I. health care professionals who are caring for the client
    II. the client's insurer
    III. the client's son or daughter
    IV. the client's immediate nuclear family

    A. I only
    B. I and II
    C. I, II and III
    D. I, II, III and IV

    1._____

2. For a nurse who provides community-based services in a senior center populated mostly by Asian-American clients, the most important preparatory skill or ability would be

    A. specialized knowledge in geriatric care
    B. mastery of how the health-care system works
    C. knowledge of the clients' culture
    D. knowledge of nutrition

    2._____

3. Which of the following is an important source of insoluble dietary fiber?

    A. Whole grain foods
    B. Sweet potatoes
    C. Oats
    D. Soybeans

    3._____

4. Factors that are known to contribute to heart disease include each of the following, EXCEPT

    A. sedentary lifestyle
    B. diabetes mellitus
    C. hyperlipidemia
    D. low triglycerides

    4._____

5. _____ is a physiological process that affects oxygenation by limiting the amount of inspired oxygen that is delivered to the alveoli.

    A. Anemia
    B. Bradycardia
    C. Airway obstruction
    D. Fever

    5._____

6. Which of the following types of data, collected during the assessment phase, would be considered subjective?

    A. The client's temperature is 98.
    B. The nurse observes that the client's face is flushed.
    C. The client states that he is nauseated and thirsty.
    D. The client's pulse is 100.

7. A nurse is designing a client teaching program that makes use of the humanistic model. The nurse's program is aimed at the client goal of

    A. becoming able to establish and maintain lifelong intimate relationships
    B. achieving her full potential
    C. gaining insight into her own behavior and being able to modify it
    D. becoming a productive member of society

8. Typically, a client's mental status is MOST effectively assessed by

    A. observing the client during the interview and examination
    B. having the client describe her mental status
    C. observing responses to a list of questions prepared in advance
    D. observing reactions to provocative questions

9. Nurses use critical thinking in the daily practice of nursing by

    A. anticipating likely medical diagnoses
    B. ensuring that there are adequate supplies on hand
    C. making conversions during medication dosage calculations
    D. setting priorities for the day

10. The oxygenation rate within body cells is regulated by the _____ gland.

    A. adrenal
    B. pineal
    C. thyroid
    D. apocrine

11. A nurse leads a group discussion on nutrition, and then asks the participants to decide on a topic of discussion for the next meeting. The nurse is representing the _____ leadership style.

    A. autocratic
    B. democratic
    C. exploitive
    D. laissez-faire

12. In order to be functional and appropriate for the situation, the nurse-client relationship must be

    A. established in an early stage by means of the nurse's statement of purpose
    B. developed from joint problem-solving work between nurse and client
    C. open-ended
    D. established by the client's willingness to accept the nurse's interventions

13. A client in a full arm cast expresses concern about preventing atrophy of the muscles in his upper arm. Assuming exercise is not contraindicated, the nurse should recommend _____ exercises.

    A. weightlifting
    B. kinetic
    C. aerobic
    D. isometric

14. An elderly client who lives at home has a history of glaucoma, for which she takes drops daily. She reports a loss of peripheral vision and an inability to adjust to darkness. Which of the following nursing diagnoses is most appropriate for her?

    A. High risk of injury related to sensory deficit
    B. High risk of injury related to impaired verbal communication
    C. High risk of injury related to lack of home safety precautions
    D. High risk for poisoning related to inadequate safeguards on medication

15. The presence of hyperemia represents the _____ stage of the inflammatory response.

    A. resolution
    B. granuloma
    C. acute vascular response
    D. chronic cellular response

16. During an assessment interview, the nurse should
    I. ask about the main problem first
    II. focus on the client, and not the signs or symptoms
    III. rely mostly on direct questions
    IV. try to avoid commentary unless it is absolutely necessary

    A. I and II
    B. I, II and IV
    C. II and III
    D. I, II, III and IV

17. Of the following clients, which would LEAST likely suffer from an imbalance in fluid, acid-base, or electrolytes?

    A. An adult with impaired cardiac function
    B. An elderly client with dementia
    C. A middle-aged client suffering from a Stage II pressure ulcer
    D. A two-year-old that has had gastroenteritis for four days

18. An overweight client with gout is discussing his diet with the nurse. During their discussion, the client should demonstrate an understanding of which foods have a high purine content. Which of the following foods would be MOST appropriate for this client?

    A. Liver
    B. Broccoli
    C. Lentils
    D. Wheat bran

19. A client has been diagnosed with terminal cancer. Shortly after the diagnosis she turns to the nurse and asks: "What should I do?" The nurse responds: "What do you think would be best for you and your family?"
    The nurse has used the therapeutic communication technique of

    A. Acknowledging
    B. Refraining
    C. Metacommunication
    D. Reflecting

20. Which of the following is NOT considered a task involved in the orientation phase of the nurse-client relationship?

    A. Exploring the client's thoughts and feelings
    B. Exploring one's own feelings and fears
    C. Clarifying the problem
    D. Structuring and developing the contract

21. One of the first clinical signs of hypovolemia associated with fluid volume deficit is

    A. tachycardia
    B. edema
    C. bradycardia
    D. shortness of breath

22. A nurse is asked to obtain an arterial blood gas from a client. Of the following, the _____ artery is the LEAST appropriate site for obtaining the blood sample.

    A. femoral
    B. brachial
    C. subclavian
    D. radial

23. Parasthesia is a condition that may in itself become the etiology for other nursing diagnoses, such as

    A. knowledge deficit
    B. fibromyalgia
    C. dehydration
    D. risk for injury

24. A client diagnosed with acute pain may exhibit the defining characteristic of

    A. weight change
    B. sympathetic nervous system responses
    C. depression
    D. sleep pattern changes

25. A food label contains the following information:
    2 grams of protein
    12 grams of fat
    15.5 grams of carbohydrate
    Using the 4-4-9 method, the nurse calculates the number of total calories to be

    A. 36
    B. 97
    C. 178
    D. 256

KEY (CORRECT ANSWERS)

1.	A	11.	B
2.	C	12.	B
3.	A	13.	D
4.	D	14.	A
5.	C	15.	C
6.	C	16.	B
7.	B	17.	C
8.	A	18.	B
9.	D	19.	D
10.	C	20.	B

21.	A
22.	C
23.	D
24.	B
25.	C

TEST 2

DIRECTIONS: Each question or incomplete statement is followed by several suggested answers or completions. Select the one that BEST answers the question or completes the statement. *PRINT THE LETTER OF THE CORRECT ANSWER IN THE SPACE AT THE RIGHT.*

1. Which of the following is an example of palliative surgery?

   A. Vascular grafting
   B. Nephrectomy
   C. Laparatomy
   D. Nerve block

2. A client has a respiratory disease that causes a chronic lack of oxygen. The nurse would need to expect and be most watchful for

   A. peripheral edema
   B. wheezing upon exhaling
   C. flushed skin
   D. clubbing of the digits

3. In reviewing the file of a client who is scheduled for an IV pyelogram, which of the following should receive the nurse's special attention?

   A. Hypertension
   B. Iodine allergy
   C. Diabetes mellitus
   D. Latest bowel movement

4. Which of following is NOT an advantage associated with the use of closed questions in interviewing a client?

   A. Greater potential for revealing a client's emotional state
   B. Ease of documentation
   C. Less skill required of the interviewer
   D. More effective control of answers

5. Of the possible complications associated with blood transfusion, the most serious is

   A. allergic reaction
   B. fever
   C. hemolysis
   D. dizziness

6. Which of the following cranial nerves is NOT assessed by evaluating the eyes and vision?

   A. First
   B. Third
   C. Fifth
   D. Sixth

7. A 78-year-old client is brought to the emergency department after suffering vomiting and diarrhea for the last 48 hours. During the nursing assessment, the nurse observes that the client's skin is dry and can be tented, and that the client complains of an itching sensation. In developing a plan of care for the client, the most appropriate diagnosis would be

    A. risk for fall related to sensory deficit, as manifested by prolonged diarrhea and vomiting
    B. risk for fluid volume deficit related to prolonged diarrhea and vomiting
    C. risk for fluid volume excess related to prolonged diarrhea and vomiting
    D. nutrition imbalanced: less than body requirements, related to prolonged diarrhea and vomiting

8. A client who is several days post-surgery complains that none of his family has been to see him since the operation. The nurse responds: "That was your son who was here just this morning, wasn't it – The man who brought those flowers?"
The type of therapeutic communication technique being used by the nurse is

    A. reflection
    B. focusing
    C. clarifying
    D. confrontation

9. Each of the following is a factor that commonly contributes to constipation, EXCEPT

    A. anxiety or stress
    B. decreased activity level
    C. low dietary fiber
    D. routine use of laxatives

10. The most significant contributing factor in cardiac disease is

    A. hypotension
    B. congenital heart defects
    C. alcohol abuse
    D. atherosclerosis

11. Clients are often encouraged to perform deep breathing exercises after surgery, in order to

    A. counteract respiratory acidosis
    B. increase cardiac output
    C. expand residual volume
    D. increase blood volume

12. Which of the following hormones acts to preserve sodium ions in the body's cells?

    A. Thyrocalcitonin
    B. Androstenone
    C. Cortisone
    D. Aldosterone

13. Which of the following is NOT an example of tertiary care?

    A. Neurosurgery
    B. Promoting workplace safety
    C. Hospice care
    D. Burn care

14. A client has died. Because proper handling of a client's body after death is an important intervention, the nurse should

    A. cover the client completely with a sheet before family members are allowed into the room
    B. apply makeup, jewelry, and any other accessories that the person wore in life before allowing the family into the room
    C. make sure the body looks as clean and natural as possible
    D. leave the body exactly as it was at the moment of death until a physician has arrived to formalize the death pronouncement

15. The nurse is meeting a new client. Which of the following would be MOST effective in initiating the nurse-client relationship?

    A. Asking the client why she was brought to the hospital.
    B. Explaining the purpose of and plan for the relationship
    C. Waiting until the client indicates a readiness to establish a relationship.
    D. Describing her family background, and then asking the client to do the same.

16. Together, a nurse and a client devise a nursing care plan with one goal being the maintenance of adequate fluid volume. The achievement of this goal can most accurately be measured by

    A. auscultation for heart and vascular sounds
    B. palpating for skin turgor, pulse, and heart rhythm
    C. monitoring bowel elimination patterns
    D. monitoring serum glucose

17. Nursing care and treatment of pressure sores is executed under each of the following general guidelines or recommended practices, EXCEPT the

    A. use of alcohol to clean and dress sores
    B. frequent repositioning of the client
    C. tissue sampling from infected sores
    D. application of cornstarch to the bedsheet

18. Clients should be screened for tuberculosis every

    A. six months
    B. year
    C. 2 years
    D. 5 years

19. Which of the following represents a primary source of data during the assessment phase of the nursing process?

    A. The client states that she has been suffering from intermittent dizzy spells.
    B. The client's spouse says the she has seemed severely fatigued lately.
    C. The client's chart documents a history of epilepsy.
    D. The client's temperature is 99° F.

20. A client with a broken left hand is awaiting an X-ray. Which of the following nonpharmacological interventions is most appropriate to help the client reduce pain prior to the procedure?

    A. Applying ice directly over the break
    B. Turning of the lights and eliminating other sensory stimuli
    C. Applying ice to the left elbow
    D. Applying warmth directly over the break

21. A nurse is planning an educational program on the detection of cancer, to be presented at a community clinic. Which of the following elements is LEAST likely to help address the various learning styles of the clients?

    A. A lecture
    B. Specific examples/case studies
    C. Audiovisuals
    D. Collaborative activities

22. Which of the following is an example of an outcome evaluation?

    A. A review of nursing documentation for compliance with institutional standards
    B. A survey to analyze staffing patterns
    C. Checking a client's temperature before administering a new medication
    D. An audit that records the number of postoperative infections

23. Which of the following tasks is part of the working phase of the nurse-client relationship?

    A. Identifying client problems
    B. Establishing trust
    C. Developing a plan for interaction
    D. Reviewing progress and attainment of goals

24. Which of the following is the body's mechanism for preventing pressure sores?

    A. third-space movement
    B. ischemia
    C. vasoconstriction
    D. vasodilation/hyperemia

25. If a client is hearing-impaired, the nurse should establish and maintain therapeutic communication by

    A. learning sign language
    B. using an interpreter
    C. using simple sentences
    D. orienting the client to sounds in the environment

KEY (CORRECT ANSWERS)

1. D		11. A
2. D		12. D
3. B		13. B
4. A		14. C
5. C		15. A
6. A		16. B
7. B		17. A
8. C		18. C
9. A		19. A
10. D		20. C

21. A
22. D
23. A
24. D
25. C

TEST 3

DIRECTIONS: Each question or incomplete statement is followed by several suggested answers or completions. Select the one that BEST answers the question or completes the statement. *PRINT THE LETTER OF THE CORRECT ANSWER IN THE SPACE AT THE RIGHT.*

1. A nurse asks a client: "What kind of abdominal pain are you feeling today?" What kind of assessment is being performed?

    A. Time-lapsed
    B. Problem-focused
    C. Initial
    D. Emergency

    1.____

2. A client has been placed on a high-fiber diet. Which of the following foods would be LEAST likely to contribute to the diet?

    A. Green peppers
    B. Cheese
    C. Apples
    D. Wheat bread

    2.____

3. A "chronic" illness is generally defined as one that lasts for more than

    A. six weeks
    B. 3 months
    C. 6 months
    D. 1 year

    3.____

4. Which of the following is NOT a sign of cardiac arrest?

    A. Crepitations auscultated in lungs
    B. No carotid pulse
    C. Dilated pupils
    D. Apnea

    4.____

5. For a client who is admitted with gastrointestinal bleeding, one of the earliest and most important blood tests will be the

    A. complete blood count
    B. Coombs test
    C. arterial blood gases
    D. lipid panel

    5.____

6. A nursing care plan for a client with a diagnosis of chronic pain related to compression of the spinal nerves involves two goals: the client will achieve a sense of pain relief within 1 month, and the client will perform self-care measures with less discomfort on self-report within 14 days. Which of the following would be an appropriate evaluation of the effectiveness of the care plan?

    A. Observing whether client has returned to social activities within 14 days
    B. Observing the client's facial expression in response to the application of localized heat
    C. Observing client's freedom of movement and facial expressions for signs of discomfort
    D. Asking if client's pain has remained localized within initially described boundaries

    6.____

7. In planning client teaching, the nurse's instruction should be most significantly guided by the knowledge that

   A. each client has unique learning needs
   B. a client's cultural background is the most important factor in determining his or her learning needs
   C. all clients share the same basic learning needs
   D. a client's learning needs are most strongly correlated with his or her life stage

8. One of the goals of a nursing care plan is for a client to return to within 10 percent of his ideal body weight. Each of the following would be an appropriate outcome to go along with this goal, EXCEPT

   A. the client loses 2 kg per week
   B. the client gains 2 kg per week
   C. the client verbalizes positive feelings about weight loss or gain
   D. the client selects appropriate foods to facilitate weight gain or loss

9. A client is recovering from a stroke and is aphasic. To establish and maintain therapeutic communication with this client, the nurse should

   A. ask brief questions that require "yes" or "no" answers
   B. be sure to provide some introductory language before each procedure or activity
   C. make as many decisions as feasible for the client, to avoid agitating her
   D. speak very slowly and enunciate clearly

10. A client is semiconscious and likely to obstruct her own airway with her tongue. If the client requires respiratory intubation and there are no contraindications, a(n) _____ tube should be used.

    A. oropharyngeal
    B. endotracheal
    C. tracheostomy
    D. nasopharyngeal

11. A nurse asks a client to close his eyes, and then places a spoon in his palm and asks the client to identify the object. Which evaluation is the nurse performing?

    A. Stereognosis
    B. Tactile spatial acuity
    C. Texture discrimination
    D. Proprioception

12. A 38-year-old woman has a diagnosis of nocturia, probably caused by pregnancy. The nurse should recommend that the client

    A. restrict fluid intake in evening and nighttime hours
    B. consult a urologist
    C. make use of a nighttime alarm to alert her when an episode is occurring
    D. avoid eating citrus fruits

13. A doctor has ordered that a client take 6 ml of a medication in solution. The nurse's equipment is marked for fluid ounces (oz). How many ounces should the nurse administer?

    A. 0.2
    B. 0.8
    C. 1.2
    D. 2.4

14. A nurse is assessing a new client for possible impairment of verbal communication. Each of the following should be a component of the assessment, EXCEPT

    A. vision
    B. level of education
    C. hearing
    D. cognitive function

15. While recovering from surgery, a client avoids eye contact with the attending nurse, both while being cared for and when speaking. This is most likely a sign that the client is feeling

    A. ashamed
    B. fearful
    C. angry
    D. weak and defenseless

16. In nurse-client communication, which of the following variables is an emotional/psychological barrier to effective reception of a message?

    A. Using one's personal experience or frame of reference in interpreting
    B. Lack of context
    C. Distorting the message to comply with one's own expectations
    D. Insufficient vocabulary

17. Total parenteral nutrition (TPN) is usually contraindicated in clients whose gastrointestinal tracts are functional within _____ following an illness, surgery, or trauma.

    A. 24 hours
    B. 3 to 5 days
    C. 7 to 10 days
    D. 1 month

18. A client is undergoing oxygen therapy. The nurse can most effectively evaluate the effectiveness of this therapy by observing changes in

    A. blood volume
    B. serum electrolyte values
    C. arterial blood gases
    D. respiration

19. Which of the following nursing skills is most likely to be required during the pre-interaction phase of the nurse-client relationship?

    A. Analyzing one's one strengths and limitations
    B. Exploring relevant stressors
    C. Overcoming resistance behaviors
    D. Establishing trust

20. A nurse is instructed to give an IM injection into the ventrogluteal muscle. Each of the following would be a landmark used for this procedure, EXCEPT the

    A. lateral femoral condyle
    B. iliac crest
    C. greater trochanter
    D. anterior superior iliac spine

21. A nurse observes that a client's stool is green, loose, and has a strong odor. Based on this assessment, the next step of the nursing process that should be implemented is

    A. evaluating
    B. assessing
    C. implementing
    D. diagnosing

22. The main consequence of repeated vomiting is

    A. fluid and electrolyte loss
    B. dental caries
    C. metabolic alkalosis
    D. sleep disorder

23. Of the following medical conditions, which is most appropriate for the use of a nursing critical pathway?

    A. Knee replacement surgery
    B. Polyuria associated with pregnancy
    C. Viral infection acquired during travel
    D. Ear blockage by impacted cerumen

24. Coping or defense mechanisms that are used by clients include each of the following EXCEPT

    A. projection   B. reinvention
    C. compensation   D. denial

25. A client who recently suffered a herniated spinal disc complains of pain in her foot. During the nursing assessment, the nurse discovers no problems with the foot. The client's pain is best described as

    A. referred   B. neuropathic
    C. phantom   D. somatic

KEY (CORRECT ANSWERS)

1. B	11. A
2. B	12. A
3. B	13. A
4. A	14. B
5. A	15. D
6. C	16. C
7. A	17. C
8. C	18. C
9. A	19. A
10. A	20. A

21. D
22. A
23. A
24. B
25. A

_____

EXAMINATION SECTION
TEST 1

DIRECTIONS: Each question or incomplete statement is followed by several suggested answers or completions. Select the one that BEST answers the question or completes the statement. *PRINT THE LETTER OF THE CORRECT ANSWER IN THE SPACE AT THE RIGHT.*

1. Multiphasic screening, now adopted by many health departments, is BEST defined as a

   A. new method of testing vision
   B. case finding procedure combining tests for several diseases
   C. combined vision and hearing test
   D. new method of cancer detection

2. Of the following statements that a nurse might make to a patient ill with cancer who says, *I don't think I'll ever get better. When the pain comes, I'm afraid I'll die before anyone gets here,* the one which would be MOST appropriate is:

   A. I wouldn't worry about that. People do not die because of pain.
   B. Of course you'll get better. You look much better than you did the last time I was here.
   C. You should try to have someone here with you and not be alone. Then you won't be afraid.
   D. I think I understand how you feel, but why do you think you won't get better?

3. In an epidemiological study of a disease, the one of the following steps which would usually NOT be included is

   A. collecting and compiling data on the incidence, prevalence, and trends of the disease
   B. reviewing the *natural history* of the disease
   C. making a sociological study of the community in which the disease is prevalent
   D. defining gaps in knowledge and developing hypotheses on which to base further investigation

4. Adequate lighting in the school is an important part of the sight conservation program. The school nurse familiar with standards for classroom lighting should know that the RECOMMENDED illumination on each desk for ordinary classroom work is _____ candles.

   A. 20-foot   B. 35-foot   C. 50-foot   D. 75-foot

5. The relation of fluorine to dental health has been the subject of extensive study for many years.
   Of the following statements concerning the relation of fluorine to dental caries, the one which is CORRECT is that

   A. mass medication by fluorine is now accepted as the best means of treating and curing dental caries
   B. fluoridation of water supplies, though effective, is too expensive for wide usage
   C. fluoridation is effective only in children born in areas in which fluoridation exists
   D. fluoridation prevents dental caries but does not treat or cure it

6. There are measures which are effective in the prevention of diabetes in those with an hereditary disposition.
   Of the following, the one which has the GREATEST value as a preventive measure is
   A. preventing acute infection
   B. preventing obesity
   C. avoidance of emotional stress
   D. avoidance of marriage with a known diabetic

7. The basis of a program of *natural childbirth* is to
   A. prevent or dispel fear through education in the physiology of pregnancy
   B. reduce premature births and the complications of pregnancy
   C. reduce the maternal and neonatal mortality rates
   D. prepare the mother's body for the muscular activity of delivery

8. The one of the following statements which is CORRECT concerning retrolental fibroplasia is that it is a
   A. blood dyscrasia
   B. condition occurring in Rh negative infants whose mothers are Rh positive
   C. condition causing blindness in premature infants
   D. complication of congenital syphilis

9. Of the following factors, the one which is MOST important in maintaining optimum health in the older age group is
   A. regular medical supervision for early recognition and treatment of minor symptoms
   B. economic independence which gives a feeling of security
   C. avoidance of all emotional tensions
   D. adjustment of the environment to prevent physical and mental strain

10. The MOST outstanding result of antibiotic therapy in the treatment of syphilis has been to
    A. reduce the toxic effect of treatment
    B. shorten the treatment period
    C. prevent a relapse
    D. prevent late complications

11. To achieve the most effective and economical case finding for tuberculosis, mass examinations should be conducted PRIMARILY for
    A. infants under one year
    B. industrial workers
    C. elementary school students
    D. pre-school age group

12. Though tuberculosis occurs in all age groups, there is a certain period of life when individuals have the greatest resistance to the infection.
    That period is
    A. under one year of age
    B. between 3 years and puberty
    C. between 15 and 35 years of age
    D. between 25 and 40 years of age

13. Drug therapy for tuberculosis has proven to be an important tool in the control of the disease in its active stage.
    Of the following, the one which has had the MOST satisfactory results to date in that fewer patients develop resistance to the drug and the incidence of drug toxicity is reduced is 13.____

    A. para-amino-salicylic acid (P.A.S.) in combination with streptomycin
    B. dihydro-streptomycin
    C. streptomycin in combination with promine
    D. penicillin

14. Studies have indicated that the use of streptomycin in the treatment of tuberculosis has GREATEST value in 14.____

    A. recently developed pneumonic or exudative lesions
    B. long standing infections which have been resistant to other therapies
    C. military T.B.
    D. meningeal T.B.

15. The PARTICULAR effectiveness of chemotherapeutic agents in the treatment of pulmonary tuberculosis is that they 15.____

    A. are important adjuncts to surgery
    B. inhibit the growth of the bacillus
    C. heal lesions rapidly
    D. render the patient non-infectious

KEY (CORRECT ANSWERS)

1. B	6. B
2. D	7. A
3. C	8. C
4. A	9. A
5. D	10. B

11. B
12. B
13. A
14. A
15. B

TEST 2

DIRECTIONS: Each question or incomplete statement is followed by several suggested answers or completions. Select the one that BEST answers the question or completes the statement. *PRINT THE LETTER OF THE CORRECT ANSWER IN THE SPACE AT THE RIGHT.*

1. The CHIEF shortcoming of chemotherapeutic agents in the treatment of pulmonary tuberculosis is

    A. their prohibitive cost in any long-term treatment
    B. the toxic effects which follow their use
    C. that their use is limited to early cases
    D. the development of bacterial resistance by the host

    1.____

2. Though precise knowledge concerning the optimum duration of chemotherapy in treating pulmonary tuberculosis is lacking, the present APPROVED practice is

    A. continued uninterrupted treatment until the sputum is negative
    B. short courses of treatment with rest periods in between
    C. continued treatment for a minimum of 12 months
    D. continued treatment for one year after a negative sputum and cultures are obtained

    2.____

3. A community program for the control of tuberculosis must include school children and school personnel if it is to be a success.
   Of the following statements, the one which BEST represents expert opinion on the use of B.C.G. vaccine in the school program for tuberculosis control is that

    A. through immunization of all school children it serves as an important control measure
    B. its chief value is that it is an inexpensive and rapid method of case finding
    C. it would nullify the subsequent use of the tuberculin test which is the best case finding method for schools
    D. it is a valuable diagnostic method which would reduce the evidence of contact with active cases

    3.____

4. Nutritional deficiencies are a common problem in geriatrics.
   The dietary adjustment usually necessary to maintain PROPER nutrition for the average person in the older age group is

    A. increased proteins and vitamins
    B. elimination of fats
    C. increased carbohydrates
    D. elimination of roughage

    4.____

5. The death rate from cancer can be reduced by early diagnosis and treatment. It is important, therefore, for the nurse to assist in case finding.
   She should know that, of the following sites, the one which the GREATEST incidence of cancer in women occurs is the

    A. mouth   B. skin   C. breast   D. rectum

    5.____

6. Many cancers appear to develop when pre-existing abnormal conditions and changes in the tissue are present.
   Of the following, the one which is at present considered PRECANCEROUS is

   A. fibroid tumor
   B. chronic cervicitis
   C. fat tissue tumor
   D. sebaceous cyst

7. The diagnosis of cancer by examination of isolated cells in body secretions is known as

   A. biopsy
   B. aspiration technique
   C. histological diagnosis
   D. Papanicolaou smear

8. Of the following statements concerning our present knowledge of the etiology of human cancer, the one which is TRUE is that

   A. there is definite evidence that some cancers are caused by a virus
   B. some types of cancer are definitely contagious
   C. there is a strong possibility that cancer is transmitted from mother to baby in utero
   D. so many factors are involved that the discovery of a single cause is unlikely

9. The National Venereal Disease Control Program carried on by the Public Health Service of the U.S. Government is concerned PRIMARILY with

   A. promoting medical programs to provide early effective treatment of infected individuals
   B. a national program of education in the prevention of venereal diseases
   C. distribution of free drugs to physicians for the treatment of venereal disease
   D. providing funds for the education of physicians and nurses in the treatment and care of venereal disease

10. Of the following, the one which is of GREATEST importance in the prevention of poliomyelitis is to

    A. build up resistance with proper diet
    B. keep away from crowds during periods when the disease is prevalent
    C. immunize with gamma globulin
    D. adopt general public health measures for the protection of food and water

11. Of the following statements concerning the present status of chemotherapy in the treatment of cancer, the one which is TRUE is:

    A. Results to date indicate it may soon surpass radiation and surgery as an effective cure
    B. It has not proven effective except in cases where early diagnosis was made
    C. It must be used in conjunction with radiation or surgery
    D. It inhibits the growth of certain types of cancer and prolongs life but is not effective as a cure

12. The W.H.O. Regional Organization for Europe has set up a long-term plan for European health needs.
    Of the following activities, the one which is NOT planned as a major activity is

A. coordinating health policies in European countries
B. promoting improved service through demonstration of an ideal health program in one country
C. promoting professional and technical education for health workers in the member countries
D. providing for exchange of services among member nations

13. A health problem becomes the concern of public health authorities when the incidence is great and the mortality rate high.
In terms of this statement, of the following problems, the one which should be a PRIMARY concern is

A. venereal diseases in young adults
B. tuberculosis
C. tropical diseases among ex-servicemen and their families
D. degenerative diseases of middle and later life

14. Of the following, the one which is now considered to be the MOST common mode of transmission of poliomyelitis is

A. infected insects
B. contaminated water
C. personal contact
D. infected food

15. The incubation period for infantile paralysis is

A. usually 7 to 14 days, but may vary from 3 to 35 days
B. not known
C. one week
D. usually 48 hours, but may vary from 1 to 7 days

KEY (CORRECT ANSWERS)

1. D
2. C
3. C
4. A
5. C
6. B
7. D
8. D
9. A
10. B
11. D
12. B
13. D
14. C
15. A

EXAMINATION SECTION
TEST 1

DIRECTIONS: Each question or incomplete statement is followed by several suggested answers or completions. Select the one that BEST answers the question or completes the statement. *PRINT THE LETTER OF THE CORRECT ANSWER IN THE SPACE AT THE RIGHT.*

1. Euphoria is a state of

    A. depression B. elation C. ideation D. frustration

2. Salts affecting acidity or alkalinity of protoplasm have the effect of

    A. osmosis
    B. condensation
    C. reduction
    D. buffer action

3. Cystitis means inflammation of the

    A. kidneys B. cystic duct C. bladder D. urethra

4. A vesicant is an agent that is used to produce

    A. fever B. relaxation C. lower pulse rate D. blisters

5. An ailment found *only* in older people is

    A. maniac depression
    B. dementia praecox
    C. senile dementia
    D. tabes dorsalis

6. To keep a restless, semi-conscious patient from falling out of bed, we should use

    A. heavy blankets stretched at the bedside, and pinned securely
    B. metal side boards
    C. restraint belts
    D. chairs at the exposed bed side

7. It is MOST important to see that reducing diets of adolescents do NOT lack

    A. fats
    B. proteins
    C. carbohydrates
    D. simple sugars

8. For poisons, swallowed in capsule or tablet form, administer

    A. a laxative B. warmth C. an emetic D. a stimulant

9. Oysters which feed on sewage sometimes transmit

    A. rabies B. yellow fever C. malaria D. typhoid fever

10. Temperatures of 0° F affect microbes to

    A. stimulate mitosis
    B. check multiplication
    C. destroy them
    D. attenuate the cellular wall

11. The medium of infection over which the health authorities have LEAST control is

    A. insects B. food C. water D. air

12. In case of sunstroke, the position of the head is

    A. lowered, together with the shoulders
    B. elevated, together with the shoulders
    C. bent forward
    D. bent down, between the knees

13. An orthopedic aspect NOT usually found in cerebral palsy is

    A. ataxia   B. syndactylism   C. athetosis   D. rigidity

14. Encephalitis has NOT been associated with

    A. infectious illnesses   B. epidemics
    C. measles   D. drugs

15. The Sulkowitch test of the urine tests for

    A. sodium   B. potassium   C. calcium   D. chlorides

16. The presence of acetone in urine indicates faulty metabolism of

    A. proteins   B. facts   C. carbohydrates   D. minerals

17. The test which aids the physician in confirming infectious mononucleosis is

    A. urinalysis   B. Wasserman
    C. sedimentation rate   D. heterophile antibody test

18. The purpose of the therapeutic bath is to

    A. cool and refresh   B. cleanse
    C. induce sleep   D. improve appearance

19. Syphilis is transmitted to the fetus through the

    A. ovum   B. embryonic fluid   C. placenta   D. sperm

20. The permissive policy employed in some mental hospitals is associated with a(n)

    A. increase in assaultive behavior
    B. open door policy
    C. decrease in the use of physical restraint
    D. increase in the use of physical restraint

21. A nurse can be of GREATEST help to the doctor by

    A. applying mental hygiene procedures
    B. suggesting treatments
    C. recording observations accurately
    D. minimizing the patients' complaints

22. Some authorities believe that *all* pregnant women should be given gamma globulin to protect them from

    A. gonococcus   B. German measles
    C. mumps   D. chicken pox

23. BCG vaccine is used to increase resistance to

    A. poliomyelitis   B. tuberculosis
    C. smallpox   D. mumps

24. In order to prevent rickets, the diet should include

    A. carotene   B. calciferol   C. riboflavin   D. thiamin

25. To a dog bite wound, apply

    A. 2% iodine   B. concentrated boric acid
    C. carbolated vaseline   D. running water

KEY (CORRECT ANSWERS)

1.	B	11.	D
2.	D	12.	B
3.	C	13.	B
4.	D	14.	D
5.	C	15.	C
6.	B	16.	C
7.	B	17.	D
8.	C	18.	A
9.	D	19.	C
10.	B	20.	B

21. C
22. B
23. B
24. B
25. D

TEST 2

DIRECTIONS: Each question or incomplete statement is followed by several suggested answers or completions. Select the one that BEST answers the question or completes the statement. *PRINT THE LETTER OF THE CORRECT ANSWER IN THE SPACE AT THE RIGHT.*

1. To prevent constipation in the aged, we should use
    - A. enemas
    - B. phenolthaleine
    - C. mineral oil
    - D. proper diet

2. Sea food should be included in the diet at least once a week because of
    - A. religion
    - B. its iodine content
    - C. its iron content
    - D. variety appeal

3. Baking soda added during the cooking of green vegetables to brighten their color, *also* acts to
    - A. destroy vitamin content
    - B. destroy texture effect
    - C. improve vitamin content
    - D. improve flavor

4. The loop of Henle is a structural component of the
    - A. aorta
    - B. pulmones
    - C. brain
    - D. kidneys

5. At birth, the normal pulse rate per minute varies between
    - A. 80-85
    - B. 90-95
    - C. 100-115
    - D. 120-150

6. Two potential killers in the home are
    - A. octachloro and methoxypromazine
    - B. wax on milk containers and chlordane
    - C. strontium 90 and nitrogen oxides
    - D. polythylene and aminotriazole

7. Toxemia of pregnancy in diabetic mothers has been GREATLY reduced by the use of
    - A. iodine
    - B. adrenalin
    - C. hormones
    - D. ergosterol

8. The body activity that is controlled CHIEFLY by the autonomic nervous system is
    - A. coughing
    - B. peristalsis
    - C. walking
    - D. sneezing

9. The basal metabolism remains *unchanged* in a person with
    - A. nephritis
    - B. malaria
    - C. leukemia
    - D. exophthalmic goiter

10. Excess glucose is removed from the blood stream by the
    - A. gall bladder
    - B. liver
    - C. small intestine
    - D. pancreas

11. After proteins are digested, they are absorbed as
    - A. peptones
    - B. fatty acids
    - C. glycerol
    - D. amino acids

12. The membrane which does NOT form part of the eyeball is the

    A. conjunctiva   B. sclera   C. choroid   D. retina

13. Upon discovering that a school child suffers from epilepsy, a teacher should notify the

    A. principal
    B. bureau of child guidance
    C. bureau for physically handicapped
    D. department of health

14. The process which *increases* the vitamin D content of milk products is

    A. homogenization   B. condensation
    C. evaporation   D. irradiation

15. A good source of amino acids is

    A. carbohydrate   B. fat   C. protein   D. citrus foods

16. For the patient, the MOST comfortable mattress protection is a

    A. rubber draw sheet   B. plastic pad
    C. quilted pad   D. plastic contour "sheet"

17. To relieve the sensitive-skinned patient from bed pressure, use a(n)

    A. inflated mattress   B. inflated rubber ring
    C. cotton bandage ring   D. sponge rubber ring

18. A symptom of dementia praecox is

    A. extroversion   B. tic paralysis
    C. unpredictability   D. cerebral hemorrhage

19. A symptom of diabetes is

    A. oliguria   B. polyuria   C. anuria   D. hematuria

20. The disease characterized by the abnormal mitosis and development of body cells is

    A. influenza   B. Parkinson's disease
    C. carcinoma   D. Graves' disease

21. The water used in preparing a mustard plaster should be

    A. boiling   B. cold   C. tepid   D. hot

22. In ear irrigation, the external ear is straightened by pulling the pinna

    A. down and back   B. down and forward
    C. up and forward   D. up and back

23. To stimulate peristalsis, the fluid in colonic irrigation should be

    A. cool   B. lukewarm   C. warm   D. hot

24. Substituting an activity in which a person can succeed for one in which he may fail, is termed

    A. sublimation
    B. projection
    C. rationalization
    D. compensation

25. Rationalization is the result of

    A. believing what one wants to believe
    B. reflective thinking
    C. scientific thinking
    D. basing conclusions on fact

KEY (CORRECT ANSWERS)

1. D
2. B
3. A
4. D
5. D

6. D
7. C
8. B
9. A
10. B

11. D
12. A
13. A
14. D
15. C

16. C
17. A
18. C
19. B
20. C

21. C
22. D
23. A
24. D
25. A

TEST 3

DIRECTIONS: Each question or incomplete statement is followed by several suggested answers or completions. Select the one that BEST answers the question or completes the statement. *PRINT THE LETTER OF THE CORRECT ANSWER IN THE SPACE AT THE RIGHT.*

1. Delusions of persecution are *typical* of 1._____
   A. epilepsy B. regression C. schizophrenia D. paranoia

2. A person with an IQ of 85 would be classified as 2._____
   A. defective B. normal C. dull average D. borderline

3. Ultra-violet rays harm the eyes by 3._____
   A. drying out mucous
   B. enlarging the pupil
   C. spotting the cornea
   D. destroying visual purple

4. The sclera and choroid tissues are found in the 4._____
   A. ear B. heart C. eye D. stomach

5. Hypoglycemia indicates the need for the administration of 5._____
   A. adrenalin
   B. a simple sugar
   C. insulin
   D. salt

6. To reduce swelling, apply 6._____
   A. hot applications
   B. cold applications
   C. electric heating pad
   D. a snug bandage

7. The value of antihistaminic compounds lies *primarily* in their ability to 7._____
   A. prevent the spread of infection
   B. relieve the allergic manifestations
   C. lessen the number of infections
   D. immunize

8. Very hot and very cold foods, fed to a patient with acute mycardial infarction, can cause irregular heart beat by irritating the 8._____
   A. median nerve
   B. common peronal nerve
   C. deep peronal nerve
   D. vagus nerve

9. The mineral which maintains osmotic pressure in the human system is 9._____
   A. iron B. potassium C. magnesium D. sodium

10. Dishes used by a patient with a communicable disease should be 10._____
    A. boiled for 5 minutes in soapy water
    B. boiled in a creosote solution
    C. washed in clear water at 180° F.
    D. washed for 5 minutes in soapy hot water

11. Incineration of infectious material means

    A. disinfecting   B. burning   C. washing   D. boiling

12. Tachycardia is also known as

    A. high blood pressure   B. low blood pressure
    C. rapid pulse   D. slow pulse

13. Dyspnea is

    A. blurring vision   B. pain around the heart
    C. difficult breathing   D. discoloration of the skin

14. *Manifest deviation* of one eye when looking at an object is called

    A. strabismus   B. astigmatism
    C. accommodation   D. glaucoma

15. Abnormally slow pulse is referred to as

    A. tachycardia   B. intermittent
    C. arrhythmia   D. brachycardia

16. The natural source of insulin is the

    A. liver   B. thymus gland   C. pineal gland   D. pancreas

17. Dilation is a medication used in the treatment of

    A. cardiac involvement   B. multiple sclerosis
    C. grand mal   D. cerebral palsy

18. The MOST practical bed sheet is made of

    A. muslin   B. broadcloth   C. nylon   D. linen

19. Contaminated equipment should be cleared of spore formers by

    A. soaking in strong acid   B. refrigerating
    C. dessicating   D. intermittent autoclaving

20. Decubitus is another name for

    A. mental derangement   B. dyspnea
    C. decayed teeth   D. bedsore

21. Of the following, the *non-infectious* disease is

    A. hepatitis   B. poliomyelitis   C. diabetes   D. impetigo

22. The CHIEF purpose of isolating a patient is to

    A. protect others   B. prevent reinfection
    C. hasten recovery   D. provide peace and comfort

23. Excessive amounts of alcoholic beverages over a period of time

    A. hamper the production of gastric juices
    B. reduce nervous anxiety
    C. dilate the blood vessels
    D. increase mental alertness

24. In giving first-aid treatment to a person who has fainted,

    A. administer a hot beverage
    B. hold the head back and open the mouth
    C. administer aromatic spirits of ammonia
    D. lower the head below heart level

25. The law which attempts to control the distribution of drugs is the

    A. Wagner Act   B. McCarran Act
    C. Harrison Act   D. Taft-Hartley Act

KEY (CORRECT ANSWERS)

1.	D	11.	B
2.	C	12.	C
3.	D	13.	C
4.	C	14.	A
5.	B	15.	D
6.	B	16.	D
7.	B	17.	C
8.	D	18.	A
9.	D	19.	D
10.	A	20.	D

21. C
22. A
23. A
24. D
25. C

TEST 4

DIRECTIONS: Each question or incomplete statement is followed by several suggested answers or completions. Select the one that BEST answers the question or completes the statement. *PRINT THE LETTER OF THE CORRECT ANSWER IN THE SPACE AT THE RIGHT.*

1. The MOST harmful drug derived from opium is   1.____
   A. heroin   B. morphine   C. cocaine   D. codeine

2. Novocaine is derived from the   2.____
   A. coca plant   B. poppy plant
   C. hemp plant   D. ergot fungus

3. A drug which is a substitute for morphine in the treatment of drug addiction is   3.____
   A. codein   B. demerol   C. pantapon   D. methadone

4. The drug having LEAST narcotic effect per unit of weight is   4.____
   A. marijuana   B. cocaine   C. opium   D. barbiturates

5. Nissel's granules are found in the   5.____
   A. kidney   B. heart   C. brain   D. lung

6. An hypnotic drug which does NOT initiate drug addiction is   6.____
   A. dormison   B. sodium amytal
   C. sodium phenobarbital   D. seconal

7. The United States Public Health Service Hospitals for drug addicts are in the cities of   7.____
   A. Chicago, Illinois, and Detroit, Michigan
   B. Lexington, Kentucky, and Fort Worth, Texas
   C. Cleveland, Ohio, and Ames, Iowa
   D. Salina, Kansas, and Delmonte, California

8. A term meaning "far-sightedness" is   8.____
   A. hyperopia   B. nystagmus
   C. strabismus   D. myopia

9. Cholecystrography is the x-ray examination of the   9.____
   A. stomach   B. spleen   C. gall bladder   D. intestines

10. Pyelonephritis is an inflammation of the   10.____
    A. kidney   B. pancreas   C. rectum   D. mastoid

11. Pellagra results from a deficiency of   11.____
    A. ascorbic acid   B. thiamine   C. riboflavin   D. niacin

12. Cheilosis results from a deficiency of   12.____
    A. pyrodoxin   B. vitamin E   C. riboflavin   D. niacin

13. In a healthy young woman, the prenatal period is *usually* a time of 13.____
    A. well being B. semi-invalidism
    C. chronic disability D. extreme emotionalism

14. The food substance which, when absorbed by the body, is MOST likely to increase the 14.____
    colloidal osmotic pressure of the blood, is
    A. carbohydrates B. fats C. glucoses D. proteins

15. An acid ash is yielded by body oxidation of 15.____
    A. meats B. citrus fruits C. potatoes D. cream

16. A precursor of vitamin A is 16.____
    A. ergosterol B. carotene C. lysine D. pyrodoxine

17. The term describing physical symptoms that do not arise *entirely* from physical causes is 17.____
    A. organic B. psychoneurotic
    C. psychosomatic D. psychopathological

18. The mechanism of attributing one's own ideas to others is termed 18.____
    A. projection B. substitution
    C. sublimation D. rationalization

19. A child's tendency to pattern after his parents is known as 19.____
    A. identification B. projection
    C. compensation D. substitution

20. Stuttering in children *usually* originates from 20.____
    A. physical handicap B. mentally deficient parents
    C. emotional conflict D. imitation of other stutterers

21. Folic acid, used in the treatment of pernicious anemia, must be given with vitamin 21.____
    A. B_1 B. B_2 C. B_6 D. B_{12}

22. Radioactive iodine compound is fed to determine the 22.____
    A. site of red blood cell production
    B. incidence of anemia
    C. presence of cholesterol
    D. thyroid activity

23. Predisposition to epilepsy may be discovered through the use of the 23.____
    A. stethoscope B. fluoroscope
    C. encephalograph D. opthalmoscope

24. An early symptom of glaucoma is 24.____
    A. blindness B. gradual loss of side vision
    C. excessive tearing D. cataract formation

25. A kind of nervous headache *usually* periodical and confined to one side of the head is   25._____
 A. pressure   B. vertigo   C. migraine   D. traumatic

KEY (CORRECT ANSWERS)

1. A
2. A
3. D
4. A
5. C

11. D
12. C
13. A
14. D
15. A

6. A
7. B
8. A
9. C
10. A

16. B
17. C
18. A
19. A
20. C

21. D
22. D
23. C
24. B
25. C

TEST 5

DIRECTIONS: Each question or incomplete statement is followed by several suggested answers or completions. Select the one that BEST answers the question or completes the statement. *PRINT THE LETTER OF THE CORRECT ANSWER IN THE SPACE AT THE RIGHT.*

1. For terminal disinfection of thermometers, soak them in a solution of   1._____
    A. 90% alcohol   B. merthiolate
    C. mercurochrome   D. boric acid

2. A child who has been in contact with a known case of measles may be considered safe after   2._____
    A. 10 days   B. 40 days   C. 7 days   D. 21 days

3. The drug often used in shock therapy is   3._____
    A. metrazol   B. dicumerol   C. dilantin   D. insulin

4. First-aid care of a third-degree burn requires   4._____
    A. an ointment   B. a sterile dressing
    C. opening of the blisters D. an antiseptic solution

5. The usual reason why an infant spits out food is that it   5._____
    A. dislikes the unfamiliar taste
    B. prefers liquids
    C. is obstinate
    D. has not learned to swallow soft foods

6. The BEST time to introduce new foods is when the child   6._____
    A. has learned to obey
    B. understands it is good for him
    C. is very hungry
    D. is very happy

7. The patient should be kept warm because the blood then   7._____
    A. *increases* in viscosity   B. *decreases* in viscosity
    C. *decreases* in fluidity   D. *increases* in saline content

8. Pure ammonia solution is   8._____
    A. alkaline   B. acid   C. neutral   D. saline

9. In a reducing diet, use of a high protein content is recommended because protein has   9._____
    A. high satiety value   B. low caloric value
    C. low specific dynamic action D. easy availability

10. Dextrose-maltose is *valuable* in infant formulae because it increases   10._____
    A. homogenization   B. digestibility
    C. palatability   D. carbohydrate content

11. The substances that are *non-miscible* are

    A. linseed oil and lime water
    B. soap and water
    C. glycerin and alcohol
    D. olive oil and acetic acid

12. The PRIMARY host for bacteria causing undulant fever is the

    A. dog   B. goat   C. cow   D. fox

13. Blood clotting is *initiated* by

    A. fibrinogen   B. thromboplastin
    C. calcium ions   D. vitamin K

14. When using the terminal heat method in preparing baby's formula,

    A. cover utensils and boil for three minutes
    B. sterilize utensils and formula before bottling
    C. sterilize the bottles
    D. stand utensils and bottles in boiling water for thirty minutes

15. The MOST accurate way to measure liquid medicine is to use a

    A. standard teaspoon
    B. standard medicine glass
    C. glass kitchen measuring cup
    D. six-ounce drinking glass

16. In preparing an ice bag, use

    A. half ice, half water
    B. enough ice to half fill the bag
    C. enough ice to fill the bag
    D. about one pound of ice

17. Acute intoxication may be a psychosis because it produces

    A. severe loss of contact with reality
    B. intellectual limitations
    C. emotional inadequacies
    D. bodily diseases

18. The substance known as ACTH is a secretion of

    A. adrenal cortex   B. thyroid
    C. anterior pituitary   D. pancreas

19. Morphine 1/4 grain administered 45 minutes before surgery is intended to serve as a

    A. respiratory depressant   B. hemotinic
    C. diuretic   D. hypnotic

20. The tissue in which infection spreads rapidly is

    A. adipose   B. fibrous   C. areolar   D. reticular

21. Boiling in water for ten minutes will destroy   21.____

    A. non-spore forming microbes   B. spore-forming microbes
    C. spore-forming pathogens   D. pathogens

22. The temperature of the child under four years of age should be taken by   22.____

    A. mouth   B. rectum
    C. axilla   D. either by mouth or axilla

23. When putting drops into the eyes of a patient,   23.____

    A. drop them on the eyeball
    B. drop onto the lower lid
    C. use the medication in an eyecup
    D. drop them into the inner corner

24. The *safe* temperature for water in a hot-water bottle for an adult with a normal skin is   24.____

    A. 140°-145° F.   B. 120°-130° F.
    C. 100°-125° F.   D. 110°-115° F.

25. If a child does NOT eat his meal,   25.____

    A. remind him to eat
    B. amuse him while he eats
    C. remove the food until next meal time
    D. remove the food until he asks for it

KEY (CORRECT ANSWERS)

1. B   11. D
2. D   12. B
3. D   13. B
4. B   14. B
5. D   15. B

6. D   16. B
7. B   17. A
8. A   18. C
9. A   19. D
10. D   20. C

21. A
22. B
23. B
24. B
25. C

TEST 6

DIRECTIONS: Each question or incomplete statement is followed by several suggested answers or completions. Select the one that BEST answers the question or completes the statement. *PRINT THE LETTER OF THE CORRECT ANSWER IN THE SPACE AT THE RIGHT.*

1. The PRINCIPAL way in which germs enter the body is through

    A. skin breaks
    B. sex organs
    C. nose and mouth
    D. eye or ear

2. Normal feeding habits develop if parents

    A. gently force the child to eat
    B. stress good manners every meal
    C. prepare food by mashing and mixing it well
    D. offer adequate food in a matter-of-fact way, without urging

3. Fluoridation of community water is

    A. definitely unsafe
    B. still in early experimental stage
    C. safe beyond reasonable doubt
    D. harmless but of little value

4. Simple goiter may be caused by lack of

    A. calcium   B. phosphorus   C. iodine   D. sodium

5. The diet in nephritic edema should be

    A. high in vitamins and fluids
    B. low in proteins and fats
    C. high in proteins and minerals
    D. low in fluids and minerals

6. In first-aid treatment of nosebleed in a young child, permit the child to

    A. lie flat on his back
    B. sit in a chair, tip head back, apply cold compresses
    C. sit up, head forward, apply cold compress at nostrils and back of neck
    D. blow nose, then press nostrils shut

7. MOST finger stains may be removed from wall paper with

    A. benzene
    B. soap and water
    C. art gum
    D. heat and brown paper

8. The "dominating gland" or master gland of all the endocrine glands is the

    A. anterior lobe of the pituitary
    B. pineal body
    C. adrenal cortex
    D. spleen

9. A *non-communicable* disease is

    A. syphilis   B. pneumonia   C. carcinoma   D. typhus fever

10. The physiological stimulant for the respiratory center is

   A. oxygen B. calcium ions
   C. carbon dioxide D. lactic acid

11. The MINIMUM time in which dishes may be disinfected by boiling in water is

   A. 15 minutes B. 10 minutes C. 5 minutes D. 2 minutes

12. Dichloro-diphenyl-trichoroethane is used extensively because it

   A. retains residual effectiveness
   B. is non-toxic to handlers
   C. does not burn
   D. dissolves in water

13. The disease that is transmitted by an insect is

   A. diphtheria B. typhus fever
   C. scarlet fever D. poliomyelitis

14. For lumbar punctures, the needle is *usually* introduced just

   A. *above* the first lumbar vertebra
   B. *below* the last lumbar vertebra
   C. *above* the last lumbar vertebra
   D. *below* the first lumbar vertebra

15. Antigens used to stimulate active immunity are called

   A. serums B. vaccines C. inoculations D. injections

16. Keratitis is an inflammation of the

   A. cornea B. iris C. fundus D. lachrymal ducts

17. The soft part of the tooth that is susceptible to decay is the

   A. pulp B. dentine C. crown D. root

18. A child with "growing pains" should be

   A. examined physically
   B. hospitalized
   C. told to forget them
   D. watched carefully for a few weeks

19. The unit used for measuring acuity of hearing is the

   A. otometer B. decibel
   C. audiometer D. auditory ossicle

20. Inflammation of the tear sac is called

   A. dacrocystitis B. cystitis
   C. iritis D. cyclitis

21. The method advocated for treating skeletal tuberculosis includes

    A. bed rest and plenty of fresh air
    B. spinal fusion operation
    C. placing patient on a rigid frame
    D. antibiotic therapy, rest and surgery

22. A mustard plaster for an adult with a normal skin should have a mixture of mustard and flour, respectively, in the proportion of one to

    A. two B. six C. ten D. twelve

23. A child activity that encourages social contacts is a

    A. picture book
    B. sandpile
    C. soft woolly toy dog
    D. a toy piano

24. The baby's FIRST toy should be something to

    A. hold
    B. watch as it moves
    C. chew on
    D. pound

25. In illness, the importance of sunshine lies CHIEFLY in the fact that it

    A. induces relaxation
    B. supplies vitamin D
    C. increases morale
    D. is a powerful disinfectant

KEY (CORRECT ANSWERS)

1. C		11. C	
2. D		12. A	
3. C		13. B	
4. C		14. D	
5. D		15. B	
6. C		16. A	
7. C		17. B	
8. A		18. A	
9. C		19. B	
10. C		20. A	

21. D
22. B
23. B
24. B
25. D

TEST 7

DIRECTIONS: Each question or incomplete statement is followed by several suggested answers or completions. Select the one that BEST answers the question or completes the statement. *PRINT THE LETTER OF THE CORRECT ANSWER IN THE SPACE AT THE RIGHT.*

1. The nurse rubs the patient's back with alcohol in order to 1.____

    A. kill germs on the patient's skin
    B. relax the muscles and prevent bed sores
    C. speed the cure
    D. keep the patient clean

2. When a prescribed medicine is no longer required, it should be 2.____

    A. saved for the next illness
    B. disposed of in the garbage or down the drain
    C. given to another patient with a similar illness
    D. administered until all is consumed

3. The purpose of the therapeutic bath is to 3.____

    A. cool and refresh   B. cleanse
    C. induce sleep   D. improve appearance

4. The change of nutrients into protoplasm is 4.____

    A. anabolism   B. karyokinesis
    C. osmosis   D. catabolism

5. The *preferred* method for administering cough medicine is 5.____

    A. from the medicine glass   B. mixed with water
    C. from a spoon   D. through a siphon tube

6. The MOST effective means of lowering the death rate from cancer is 6.____

    A. radium treatment   B. x-ray treatment
    C. early diagnosis   D. surgery

7. The FIRST attack of rheumatic fever results in a child being 7.____

    A. immune to further attacks
    B. permanently crippled
    C. subject to further attacks
    D. certain to have heart complications

8. The hereditary disease in which blood does NOT clot properly is 8.____

    A. anemia   B. leukemia   C. hemophilia   D. amoebiosis

9. In first aid, a penetrating foreign body in the eyeball should be treated by 9.____

    A. removing the object
    B. applying a loose bandage
    C. sending the patient to a doctor
    D. applying a snug bandage

10. The effect of heat on the vasodilator is to

    A. stimulate   B. deteriorate   C. stabilize   D. inhibit

11. A stroke is a(n)

    A. cerebral hemorrhage   B. sinus thrombosis
    C. cerebral dystrophy   D. aneurism

12. Painful effects of arthritis may be caused by

    A. chilling winds
    B. toxins from a disease germ
    C. complications of an infectious disease
    D. air conditioning

13. In diabetes, the body is unable to utilize

    A. vitamins   B. proteins   C. fats   D. carbohydrates

14. The aged bed patient is likely to have bed sores because he

    A. is uncooperative
    B. lies in one position and has poor circulation
    C. limits his diet
    D. is uncomfortable

15. The thinking of an alcoholic becomes compulsive about

    A. the next drink   B. abstinence
    C. violence   D. the need for relaxation

16. The *normal* inspiration rate per minute for the healthy adult is

    A. 8-12   B. 16-20   C. 24-28   D. 30-35

17. Anemia is determined by

    A. color of skin   B. laboratory techniques
    C. undue fatigue   D. dizziness without apparent cause

18. The aged citizen is BEST cared for in

    A. the home environment
    B. old age homes
    C. hospitals for the aged
    D. a town developed for old people

19. The outside leaves of salad greens are important because they

    A. make the salad crispy   B. are larger
    C. have more color   D. contain more vitamin A and iron

20. Rubber goods should be stored in a

    A. cool dry place   B. tin container
    C. medicine cabinet   D. warm, moist place

21. Caffeine and strychnine stimulate the 21.____

    A. brain and afferent nerves
    B. brain and spinal cord
    C. autonomic ganglia and efferent nerves
    D. hepatic and pulmonary nerves

22. To get the required amount of vitamin C, consume 22.____

    A. cole slaw B. cocoa
    C. apricots   D. whole wheat bread

23. Hyperfunution of the islands of Langerhans may cause 23.____

    A. hypoliposis   B. hemorrhage
    C. hypoglycemia D. hypostalic congestion

24. Osteomalacia is 24.____

    A. bony tumor   B. softening of the bones
    C. inflammation of bone marrow D. formation of bone

25. Asphyxiation may be caused by 25.____

    A. heavy concentration of alcohol in the blood stream
    B. consuming alcohol on an empty stomach
    C. mixing more than one kind of alcoholic drink
    D. taking sedatives while drinking

KEY (CORRECT ANSWERS)

1. B		11. A	
2. B		12. B	
3. A		13. D	
4. D		14. B	
5. C		15. A	
6. C		16. B	
7. C		17. B	
8. C		18. A	
9. B		19. D	
10. A		20. A	

21. B
22. A
23. C
24. B
25. A

TEST 8

DIRECTIONS: Each question or incomplete statement is followed by several suggested answers or completions. Select the one that BEST answers the question or completes the statement. *PRINT THE LETTER OF THE CORRECT ANSWER IN THE SPACE AT THE RIGHT.*

1. An incision of the colon for the purpose of making a fistula is an operation termed 1.____
   - A. colostration
   - B. colostomy
   - C. Mikulicz operation
   - D. gastrostomy

2. "Mainliner" is a drug addict who uses the drug for 2.____
   - A. smoking
   - B. snorting
   - C. intra-muscular injection
   - D. intra-venal injection

3. Bright's disease is also called 3.____
   - A. hepatitis
   - B. nephritis
   - C. Paget's disease
   - D. otitis

4. Anodyne refers to a medication that 4.____
   - A. counteracts or removes the effect of poison
   - B. relieves pain
   - C. prevents the growth of germs
   - D. prolongs the life of red blood cells

5. Common symptoms of shock are 5.____
   - A. slow pulse, flushed skin
   - B. slow pulse, bright eyes
   - C. pale skin, bright eyes
   - D. pale, clammy skin

6. The CHIEF value of cellulose in the diet is that it 6.____
   - A. is more soluble than starch
   - B. gives bulk to the intestinal residues
   - C. is easily digested
   - D. provides an essential amino acid

7. Adult dietary protein requirements are determined PRIMARILY by 7.____
   - A. age and weight
   - B. climatic conditions
   - C. body weight in relation to age and height
   - D. muscular activity

8. The purpose of insuring regular rate of respiration is to reduce the amount of 8.____
   - A. water in the body
   - B. blood passing through the aorta
   - C. carbon dioxide in the blood
   - D. iron in the red blood cells

9. Treatment of generalized arteriosclerosis is through

   A. bed rest
   B. moderation in living
   C. drugs
   D. dealing with the aging process

10. Prolonged administration of narcotics is MOST likely to result in the

    A. need for increased dosage
    B. reduction of physical resistance
    C. development of aggressiveness
    D. addiction or craving for the drug

11. Rugs and carpets should be removed from the sick room because they

    A. collect dust and germs
    B. increase the work in cleaning
    C. produce a static when walked on
    D. present a hazard

12. The administration of narcotics in the hospital is by the

    A. doctor   B. nurse   C. pharmacist   D. aide

13. Of the following, the factor contributing MOST to apoplexy is

    A. coronary thrombosis
    B. aphasia
    C. low blood pressure
    D. high blood pressure

14. Croup responds MOST quickly to administrations of

    A. pertussin medication
    B. special diet
    C. steam inhalations
    D. restricted physical movement

15. It is CORRECT to state that enzymes

    A. are used up in chemical reactions of foods
    B. retard the process of breaking down of foods
    C. work only in acid surroundings
    D. are specific in their action

16. Of PRIME importance in training children is

    A. mild punishment
    B. scolding for deviate behavior
    C. consistency of treatment
    D. ignoring undesirable behavior

17. In the destruction of microbes, the effect of heat is to produce

    A. liquefaction
    B. asphyxiation
    C. coagulation
    D. precipitation

18. Hutchinson's teeth are an indication of

    A. rickets
    B. congenital syphilis
    C. rheumatic heart disease
    D. nutritional anemia

19. A drug often used in the prevention and treatment of motion sickness is

   A. dramamine
   B. streptomycin
   C. atropin
   D. aureomycin

20. The substance which is NOT a constituent of normal urine is

   A. ammonia   B. creatinine   C. hippuric acid   D. indican

21. To reduce fear in children, parents should

   A. extend affection
   B. explain each request
   C. keep them under close supervision
   D. provide safeguards

22. When a child is believed to be suffering with a communicable disease, it is the responsibility of the school to

   A. send him home
   B. send him to a doctor
   C. isolate him
   D. report the matter to the administrative office

23. The GREATEST production care is given to milk that is labeled

   A. pasteurized
   B. approved Grade A
   C. homogenized
   D. certified

24. Of the following, the MOST common cause of death today is

   A. cancer   B. diabetes   C. heart disease   D. pneumonia

25. Lipase converts

   A. fats into fatty acids
   B. fats into proteoses
   C. proteins into amino acids
   D. sugars into fructose

KEY (CORRECT ANSWERS)

1. B
2. D
3. B
4. B
5. D

6. B
7. C
8. C
9. B
10. D

11. D
12. B
13. D
14. C
15. D

16. C
17. C
18. B
19. A
20. D

21. A
22. A
23. D
24. C
25. A

TEST 9

DIRECTIONS: Each question or incomplete statement is followed by several suggested answers or completions. Select the one that BEST answers the question or completes the statement. *PRINT THE LETTER OF THE CORRECT ANSWER IN THE SPACE AT THE RIGHT.*

1. First aid care of a third degree burn requires

    A. oil and chalk mixture
    B. antiseptic solution
    C. sterile dressing
    D. healing ointment

2. Heat destroys bacteria by

    A. enucleation
    B. coagulating protein
    C. hemolysis
    D. making the cell wall permeable

3. The process by which digested food enters the blood stream is known as

    A. assimilation
    B. catabolism
    C. osmosis
    D. anabolism

4. The control of automatic breathing is located, in the

    A. cerebellum
    B. cerebrum
    C. amnion
    D. medulla oblongata

5. Difficulty in speaking is known as

    A. anorexia   B. amnesia   C. aphasia   D. asphyxia

6. Drug withdrawal symptoms in addicts are vomiting and changes in

    A. muscular control
    B. color of the skin
    C. nerves
    D. pupils of the eyes

7. Croup responds MOST quickly to

    A. steam inhalations
    B. a balanced diet
    C. cough syrup
    D. bed rest

8. The organ MOST commonly affected by arteriosclerosis is the

    A. brain   B. lung   C. kidney   D. heart

9. The position of the head for treatment in a case of "sun-stroke" is

    A. lowered on to the chest
    B. lowered between the knees
    C. elevated together with the shoulders
    D. elevated in erect position

10. Radioactive iodine compound is fed to a patient to determine the

    A. site of red blood cell production
    B. incidence of anemia
    C. presence of cholesterol
    D. activity of the thyroid

11. Doctors and nurses are required to treat ophthalmia neonatorium with

    A. penicillin
    B. sulfacetamide
    C. silver nitrate
    D. sulphathiozole

12. The administration of drugs in the hospital is *usually* by the

    A. doctor   B. nurse   C. pharmacist   D. aide

13. The care of the mouth thermometer after use is by *immediately*

    A. soaking for 5 minutes in an antiseptic solution
    B. soaping and rinsing alternately twice and carefully drying
    C. storing in alcohol
    D. washing under running water

14. An alcohol sponge bath reduces an elevated temperature because

    A. the odor is refreshing
    B. it removes moisture from the skin surface
    C. it absorbs heat by evaporation
    D. the sting stimulates the skin

15. In city schools, every school child MUST be immunized against

    A. whooping cough
    B. polio
    C. small pox
    D. diphtheria

16. Skeletal tuberculosis is treated by

    A. bed rest and plenty of fresh air
    B. spinal fusion surgery
    C. rigorous antibiotic therapy combined with rest and possible surgery
    D. restraint of spinal movement

17. A child with "growing pains" should be

    A. encouraged to disregard them
    B. hospitalized at once
    C. observed carefully for a week before attempting remedy
    D. sent for a physical examination

18. Some carbohydrates are required in a diabetic diet in order that

    A. sugars may be avoided
    B. fats may be oxidized
    C. loss of weight may be prevented
    D. intestinal putrefaction may be reduced

19. The diet of a 72-year-old obese woman should include *extra* quantities of

    A. proteins   B. vitamins   C. carbohydrates   D. minerals

20. ACTH is a secretion of the

    A. parathyroid
    B. adrenal cortex
    C. anterior pituitary
    D. thyroid

21. Blood clotting is *accelerated* by the administration of
    A. fibrinogen
    B. vitamin K
    C. calcium carbonate
    D. thromboplastin

22. The MOST common cause of death in the United States today is
    A. cancer
    B. heart disease
    C. diabetes
    D. pneumonia

23. A stroke is one of the effects of
    A. cerebral dystrophy
    B. aneurysm
    C. cerebral hemorrhage
    D. sinus thrombosis

24. Inability to write, due to a brain lesion, is known as
    A. agraphia
    B. aphasia
    C. aproxia
    D. anorexia

25. Marijuana is obtained from the
    A. hemp plant
    B. thorn apple
    C. coca shrub
    D. nightshade plant

KEY (CORRECT ANSWERS)

1.	C	11.	C
2.	B	12.	B
3.	C	13.	D
4.	D	14.	C
5.	C	15.	C
6.	D	16.	C
7.	A	17.	D
8.	C	18.	B
9.	C	19.	B
10.	D	20.	C

21. D
22. B
23. C
24. A
25. A

GLOSSARY OF MEDICAL TERMS (EYE, EAR, NOSE AND THROAT)

CONTENTS

	PAGE
ABDUCT ...... AUDIOMETER	1
AUDITORY CORTEX ...... COMPLAINT	2
COMPRESSION ...... EPITHELIUM	3
EQUILIBRIUM ...... FURUNCLE	4
GUSTATORY ...... INTRINSIC	5
LACERATION ...... MILLIMETER	6
MOLECULAR ...... OSTEOMYELITIS	7
OTOLARYNGOLOGIST ...... PSYCHIATRIC	8
PULMONARY ...... SPECULUM	9
SPHINCTER ...... TRAUMA	10
TRISMUS ...... VOCALIZATION	11

GLOSSARY OF MEDICAL TERMS (EYE, EAR, NOSE AND THROAT)

<u>A</u>

ABDUCT
　To draw away from the median line. When the vocal cords abduct, they separate.
ACCELERATION
　A quickening or speeding up.
ACOUSTIC
　As pertaining to sound or to the sense of hearing.
ACUTE
　Having a short and relatively severe course.
ADDUCT
　To move towards the median. When the vocal cords adduct, they come together.
ADENOIDITIS
　Inflammation of the adenoid tissue in the nasopharynx.
ALLERGEN
　The material responsible for an allergic reaction.
AMPLIFY
　The process of making larger or louder, as the increase of an auditory stimulus.
ANATOMY
　The science of the structure of the body and the relation of its parts.
ANGINA
　A severe pain.
ANGULAR
　Sharply bent; having corners or angles.
ANTIBIOTIC
　A chemical substance which has the capacity to inhibit the growth of or destroy bacteria and other microorganisms.
ANTIHISTAMINE
　Any of several drugs used to minimize an allergic reaction.
ANTISEPTIC
　A substance that will inhibit the growth and development of microorganisms.
ASCENT
　A rising up. The amount of upward slope or elevation.
ASEPTIC
　Not septic. Free from infectious material.
ASPIRATION
　The removal of fluids or debris from a cavity by means of an aspirator.
ASTHMA
　A disease marked by recurrent attacks of difficult breathing.
ATMOSPHERIC PRESSURE
　The pressure due to the weight of the earth's atmosphere, equal at sea level to about 14.7 pounds per square inch.
AUDIOMETER
　Device for testing the power of hearing.

AUDITORY CORTEX
   The sensory area of hearing located in the temporal lobe of the brain.
AURICLE
   That portion of the external ear not contained within the head.
AUTOCLAVE
   An apparatus for effecting sterilization by steam under pressure.

B

BACTERIA
   A loosely used generic name for any microorganism of the order Eubacteriales.
BACTERIAL
   Pertaining to or caused by bacteria.
BAROTRAUMA
   Injury caused by pressure, such as injury to the middle ear or sinus cavity due to difference in pressure between the atmosphere and the inside of the cavity.
BENIGN
   Not malignant.
BIFID
   Clefts into two parts or branches.
BILATERAL
   Having two sides or pertaining to two layers.

C

CANNULATION
   The insertion of a cannula into a hollow organ or body cavity.
CAUTERIZE
   To burn with a hot instrument or with a caustic substance so as to destroy tissue or prevent the spread of infection.
CELLULITIS
   Infection or inflammation of the loose subcutaneous tissue.
CENTIMETER
   A unit of measurement in the metric system. Being equal to 0.3937 inch.
CEREBRAL SPINAL FLUID
   A clear fluid contained within the cavities of and surrounding the brain and spinal cord.
CERUMEN
   The wax-like secretion found within the external auditory canal.
CHONDROMA
   A benign tumor of cartilage.
CHRONIC
   Persisting over a long period of time.
COMMINUTION
   Broken into small fragments.
COMPLAINT
   The symptom or group of symptoms about which the patient consults the physician.

COMPRESSION
  The act of pressing together to diminish volume and increase density.
CONCOMITANT
  Accompanying or joined with another.
CONGENITAL
  Existing at or before birth.
CULTURE
  The propagation of microorganisms in a special media.
CURRETAGE
  To remove by scraping.
CYCLES PER SECOND
  In audiology, the number of sound waves passing a point per second.
CYST
  A sac which contains a liquid or semisolid material.

D

DECAY
  The process of stage of decline. The decomposition of dead organic matter.
DECONGESTANT
  A drug which reduces congestion or swelling.
DEMARKATION
  Any dividing line apparent on the surface of the body, such as the boundary between normal and infected tissue.
DERMATITIS
  Inflammation of the skin.
DESCENT
  A coming down, going down, or downward motion.
DIPLOPIA
  Double vision.
DISCRIMINATION
  The ability to make or to perceive distinctions.

E

EDEMA
  The presence of abnormally large amounts of fluid in the intercellular tissue spaces of the body.
ENDOLYMPH
  The fluid contained in the membranous labyrinth of the ear.
ENOPHTHALMUS
  Abnormal retraction of the eye into the orbit.
ENTITY
  An independently existing thing; a reality.
EPISTAXIS
  Nose bleed or hemorrhage from the nose.
EPITHELIUM
  The covering of the internal and external surfaces of the body.

EQUILIBRIUM
A state of balance. A condition in which opposing forces exactly counteract each other.

ERYTHEMA
A name applied to redness of the skin produced by congestion of the capillaries. This may result in a variety of causes such as infection and trauma.

EUSTACHIAN TUBE
A slender tube between the middle ear and the pharynx which serves to equalize air pressure on both sides of the ear drum. Named after Bartolommeo Eustachio, an Italian anatomist.

EVACUATE
To make empty; to remove the contents.

EXACERBATION
An increase or recurrence in the severity of any symptom or disease.

EXCISION
An act of removing by cutting away.

EXOSTOSIS
An abnormal bony protuberance.

EXTRINSIC
Coming from or originating outside the organ or limb where found.

EXUDATE
Material such as fluid, cells, or cellular debris which has been deposited in or on tissue surfaces. This usually is the result of inflammation.

F

FIBROUS
Composed of or containing fibers.

FILAMENTOUS
Long, thread-like structures.

FIXATION
The act of holding, suturing, or fastening in a fixed position. Direction of a gaze so that the image of the object looked at falls on the fovea centralis.

FORAMEN
A natural opening or passage, especially a passage into or through a bone.

FREQUENCY
The number of vibrations made by a particle or ray per unit of time.

FUNCTIONAL HEARING LOSS
Hearing loss without an organic basis, such as malingering or psychological.

FUNGUS
A class of vegetable organisms of a low order of development which includes molds, mushrooms, and toadstools.

FURUNCLE
A painful nodule formed in the skin by bacteria which enter into the hair follicles causing a localized infection.

G

GUSTATORY
Pertaining to the sense of taste.

H

HEMATOMA
A swelling containing blood.
HERTZ
The international unit of frequency, equal to one cycle per second.
HIVES
An allergic skin condition characterized by itching, burning, and stinging during the formation of a red papular rash.
HYPERACTIVE
Abnormally increased activity.
HYPEREMIA
Redness of a part due to engorgement of blood vessels.
HYPERTENSION
Abnormally high blood pressure.
HYPERTROPHIC
The enlargement or overgrowth of an organ due to an increase in size of its cells.
HYPERVENTILATION
Abnormally rapid and deep breathing.
HYPOACTIVE
Abnormally diminished activity.
HYSTERIA
A psychoneurosis characterized by lack of control of emotions.

I

IMPREGNATE
To saturate one material with another, such as to saturate gauze with an ointment.
INBIBITION
The absorption of a liquid.
INCISION
A cut or a wound produced by cutting.
INFECTION
Invasion of the body by pathogenic microorganisms and the reaction of the tissue to their presence and to the toxins generated by the microorganisms.
INFLAMMATION
The condition into which tissues enter as a reaction to injury or infection. It is characterized by pain, heat, redness, and swelling of the area.
INTRINSIC
Situated entirely within or pertaining exclusively to a part.

L

LACERATION
  A wound made by tearing.
LARYNGITIS
  Inflammation of the larynx.
LARYNGOPHARYNX
  That portion of the pharynx lying between the upper edge of the epiglottis and the vocal cords.
LATENT
  Concealed or not yet manifest.
LATERAL
  The position of a part further from midline than another part of the same side.
LESION
  A pathologic or traumatic lack of continuity of tissue or loss of function of a part.
LEUKEMIA
  A fatal disease of the blood-forming organs characterized by a marked increase in the number of white blood cells.
LINEAR
  Pertaining to or resembling a line. Linear acceleration means acceleration in a straight line.

M

MALAISE
  A vague feeling of discomfort.
MALIGNANT
  As applied to tumors, malignant means the tendency to invade surrounding structures and the ability to spread to other parts of the body by way of the bloodstream or lymphatic channels.
MALINGERING
  The faking or exaggeration of symptoms of an illness or injury.
MALOCCLUSION
  The lack of occlusion between the maxillary and mandibular teeth which interferes with mastication.
MANIFEST
  Something which is readily evident or clear to the sight or mind.
MARSUPIALIZATION
  An operation which removes a portion of a cyst, abscess, or tumor, empties its contents, and sutures its edges to the line of incision.
MASTICATION
  The chewing of food.
MEMBRANE
  A layer of tissue which covers the surface or divides a space or organ.
MENINGITIS
  An inflammation or infection of the meningeal covering of the brain.
MICRON
  A unit of measurement equal to 1/1000th of a millimeter.
MILLIMETER
  A unit of measurement equaling 1/1000th of a meter or 0.03937 inch.

MOLECULAR
  Pertaining to molecules or a chemical combination of two or more atoms.
MORBIDITY
  The condition of being diseased or sick.
MORTALITY
  Death.
MUCOSA
  The mucous membrane covering a surface such as the membrane covering the surface of the palate or tongue.
MYRINGITIS
  Inflammation of the tympanic membrane.
MYRINGOTOMY
  An incision through the tympanic membrane.
MYRINGOPLASTY
  The surgical repair of a perforation in the tympanic membrane.

N

NECROSIS
  The death of a tissue or a part.
NEOPLASM
  Any new growth or tumor. It may be either a benign or malignant process.
NYSTAGMUS
  An involuntary rapid movement of the eyeball which may be horizontal, vertical, or rotary.

O

OBJECTIVE
  Pertaining to things which are perceptible to the senses.
OCCLUSION
  The relationship of the maxillary and mandibular teeth when in functional contact.
OINTMENT
  A semisolid preparation for external application to the body.
OLFACTION
  The sense of smell or the act of smelling.
OMINOUS
  Serving as an omen, or having a character of an evil omen.
OPEN REDUCTION
  Reduction of a fracture after exposing the fracture by an incision.
ORGANISM
  A body of living material. It may be a single cell, plant, or animal.
ORIFICE
  The entrance or outlet of any body cavity.
OSSEOUS
  Bone or bony.
OSTEOMYELITIS
  Inflammation or infection of bone.

OTOLARYNGOLOGIST
  A physician who has specialized in the surgical and medical treatment of diseases of the ear, nose, and throat.
OTORRHEA
  A discharge from the ear.
OTOTOXIC
  Pertaining to something which is toxic to the ear. Specifically, certain drugs destroy the minute sensory cells of the inner ear.

P

PARENTERAL
  Refers to medicine given by the subcutaneous, intramuscular, or intravenous route.
PARESIS
  Slight or incomplete paralysis.
PATENT
  Open, unobstructed.
PATHOGENIC
  Refers to an organism or substance capable of causing disease.
PEDIATRIC
  That branch of medicine which treats children.
PERCEPTION
  The awareness of objects or other data through the medium of the senses.
PERFORATE
  To pierce with holes.
PERIPHERY
  Away from center. Example: The finger is peripheral to the elbow.
PETROUS
  Resembling a rock. The petrous bone is so-called because of its hardness.
PHARYNGITIS
  Inflammation of the pharynx.
PHARYNX
  The tube between the posterior portion of the mouth and nose above, and the trachea and esophagus below.
PRACTITIONER
  An authorized practitioner of medicine.
PHYSIOLOGY
  The science or study of the function of living organisms.
PITCH
  The quality of sound dependent upon the frequency of vibration.
PNEUMATIZATION
  The formation of air-filled cells or cavities in tissues. Especially such formation in the temporal bone.
PROPAGATE
  To reproduce, multiply, or spread.
PROPHYLACTIC
  An agent that tends to ward off disease.
PSYCHIATRIC
  That branch of medicine which deals with disorders of the human mind.

PULMONARY
　Pertaining to the lungs.
PURULENT
　Consists of or contains pus.

Q

QUALITATIVE
　Having to do with the quality of something.
QUANTITATIVE
　Having to do with the quantity of something, capable of being measured.

R

RAPPORT
　A close or sympathetic relationship.
RAREFACTION
　The condition of being or becoming less dense.
REVOLUTION
　A turning or spinning motion of a body or thing around a center axis.
RHINORRHEA
　The discharge of material from the nose.
RHINOSCOPY
　The examination of the nasal passages.
ROENTGENOGRAM
　The film produced by x-ray.

S

SALINE
　A solution of salt and water.
SALPINGITIS
　Inflammation of a tube. For example: eustachian salpingitis.
SAPROPHYTE
　An organism that lives on dead or decaying organic matter.
SEBACEOUS GLANDS
　Glands which secrete a greasy lubricating substance.
SEPTOPLASTY
　An operation to straighten the nasoseptum.
SEROUS
　Material which resembles blood serum.
SIMPLE FRACTURE
　A fracture of bone in which the bone does not protrude through the skin.
SPECULUM
　An appliance used to view a passage or cavity in the body. Examples include nasal and ear speculums.

SPHINCTER
   A ring-like band of muscle fibers that constrict a passage or close a natural orifice.
SPONDEE
   Two heavily accented syllables.
SPONTANEOUS
   Occurring without external influence. Such as the spontaneous recovery from an illness.
STAPEDECTOMY
   An operation which includes the removal of the stapes and its footplate, and placement of some form of prosthesis, such as wire, to take the place of the stapes.
STEROID
   A group of compounds that resemble cholesterol. For the most part, these drugs are used for their anti-inflammatory effect. Cortisone is the best known example of this group of medications.
STIMULUS
   Any agent, act, or influence that produces a reaction in the receptor.
STOMATITIS
   Inflammation of the oral mucosa.
STRIDOR
   The wheezing noise present on inspiration or expiration when partial obstruction of the larynx is present.
SUBCUTANEOUS
   Situated or occurring beneath the skin.
SUBEPITHELIAL
   Situated beneath the epithelium.
SUBJECTIVE
   Pertaining to or perceived only by the affected individual.
SUBMUCOUS RESECTION
   Excision of the cartilage of the nasoseptum.
SUPINE
   The position assumed when lying on the back.
SYMPTOM
   Any change in a patient's condition indicative of some bodily or mental state.
SYSTEMIC
   Pertaining to or affecting the body as a whole.

T

THERMAL
   Pertaining to, characterized by heat.
THRESHOLD
   That value at which a stimulus minimally produces a sensation.
TINNITUS
   A buzzing or ringing noise in the ears.
TRANSUDATE
   A fluid substance which has passed through a membrane or has been extruded from a tissue as a result of inflammation.
TRAUMA
   A wound or injury.

TRISMUS
   Difficulty in opening the mouth due to mascular spasms, pain, or disturbance of the 5th cranial nerve.
TUMOR
   Any swelling. It may indicate either inflammation, infection, or neoplasm.
TYMPANOPLASTY
   Surgical reconstruction of the hearing mechanism of the middle ear.

U

UNILATERAL
   Affecting one side only.

V

VENEREAL
   Due to or propagated by sexual intercourse.
VERTIGO
   A hallucination of movement. A sensation as if the external environment is revolving around the patient, or as if the patient were revolving in space.
VESICULATION
   Small circumscribed elevations of epithelium containing a serous liquid.
VIRUS
   One of a group of minute infectious agents which are too small to be seen under a microscope.
VOCALIZATION
   The act of making a sound through the mouth.

www.ingramcontent.com/pod-product-compliance
Lightning Source LLC
Chambersburg PA
CBHW082206300426
44117CB00016B/2686